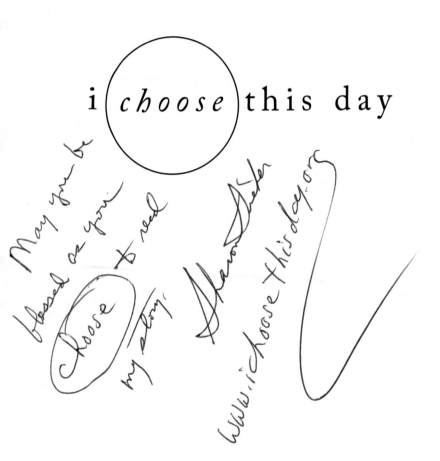

i (choose) this day

May you be blessed as you (choose) to read my story!

Sharon Slater

www.ichoosethisday.org

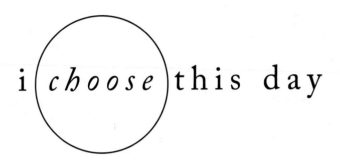

i (*choose*) this day

"Mournings and *Miracles* of Adoption"

SHARON FIEKER

with contributions by Lori Smith

TATE PUBLISHING *&* *Enterprises*

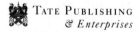
TATE PUBLISHING
& Enterprises

I Choose This Day: Mournings and Miracles of Adoption
by Sharon Fieker
Copyright © 2006 by Sharon Fieker. All rights reserved.
Visit www.tatepublishing.com for more information.

Scripture quotations marked "NIV" are taken from the *Holy Bible, New International Version* ®, Copyright © 1973, 1978, 1984 by International Bible Society. Used by permission of Zondervan Publishing House. All rights reserved.

Scripture quotations marked "NLT" are taken from the *Holy Bible, New Living Translation*, Copyright © 1996. Used by permission of Tyndale House Publishers, Inc. All rights reserved.

Book design copyright © 2006 by Tate Publishing, LLC. All rights reserved.
Cover design by Sommer Buss
Interior design by Taylor Rauschkolb

Published in the United States of America

ISBN: 1–5988653–6-6

06.09.22

dedication

This book is dedicated with everlasting love and thanks to my daughter Lori who gave me a reason to come out from under a shell of protection with a radiant smile.

and in loving memory to

My mom who died in March 2003. Meeting her granddaughter Lori was one of the many joys in her life. Mom proofed my first draft, and she was one of my strongest encouragers for getting this story published.

and

My niece Cindy who died in June 2006. She was like a daughter to me.

acknowledgments

Special thanks go to my family and friends for being there for me through the ups and the downs, for helping me to get by, for encouraging me, and for holding me accountable to write this book.

In appreciation for the time and willingness to help me in editing my manuscript, I acknowledge and thank my daughter, her mom, my sisters, and my niece Norma. I also thank my friends, Kathy Barber, Geri Bowen, Carol Deeds, LaWanka Mallard, Lynn Morrissey, Shirley Smith, Kathy Wrinkle, Patty Kennedy, and Ann Floyd.

My hope is for those in the Adoption Triad and those in unplanned pregnancies to benefit from reading about my experiences under a shell of protection.

table of contents

foreword

Sharon's book reveals mystery, insight, and God's miracles surrounding her unplanned pregnancy. Her story is inspirational and will serve as a reminder that God has a perfect plan for each of us, and He will bring it to pass. Sharon is now a leader of adoption awareness in Southwest Missouri. She coordinates an adoption triad that is a support group for all parties touched by adoption. Additionally, she has been both a volunteer and an employee at the Pregnancy Care Center where she has inspired many women facing the difficult circumstances of an untimely pregnancy. Because Sharon made an adoption plan for her daughter with whom she now has a meaningful relationship, her story is one for anyone making difficult choices as a result of an unexpected pregnancy. Those having difficulties because of past choices they've made or from choices made for them can also benefit from this book.

Cindi Boston

Executive Director, Pregnancy Care Center, Springfield, MO.

preface

The LORD is my rock, my fortress and my deliverer; my
God is my rock, in whom I take refuge. He is my shield
and the horn of my salvation, my stronghold.
(Psalm 18:2, NIV)

*I*n November 1994, I wrote a college term paper called "The Shell Within" for a Death & Dying class. Having collected turtles for over 30 years, I used the analogy of a turtle to explain unresolved grief. A turtle goes into its shell when danger approaches and hides until everything appears safe.

After placing my baby daughter for adoption in August 1969, I chose to hide under a shell of protection for the next 25 years and not discuss her. Burying that part of my life deep inside, I allowed myself time to think about her only when I was safe at home alone where others could not see my pain. Sharing with others the hurts, struggles, and joys of my life has been healing for me. Turning to God for His shell of protection in July 1993, two years before my daughter found me, was the beginning of a new and rewarding life for me.

We all make choices, and this book shows the choices I made when faced with an unplanned pregnancy.

never lose hope

Now faith is being sure of what we hope for
and certain of what we do not see.
(Hebrews 11:1, NIV)

On Thursday, February 2, 1995, I received a phone call that changed my life forever. I had hoped for such a call for many years.

"Is this Sharon Fiker?"

"Yes." I thought the caller was a solicitor because she didn't pronounce my name as Feeker. She didn't waste time getting to the point:

"My name is Marcia. I'm a social worker in Kansas City. In August 1969, you gave birth to a baby girl and gave her up for adoption. She wants to see you now."

Nearly dropping the phone, I burst out crying.

"I know this has come as a shock to you," she said. "Maybe I should call back later after you've had time to adjust."

"No. I want to hear everything now," I said. I was afraid she would hang up and never call back.

After watching talk shows and movies about adoption reunions on television, I had always wondered how I would react should I receive such a call. How would I ever explain a daughter to my friends? Since I had never married nor told my friends about her, what would they think about me? The stigma of the late '60s had stuck with me throughout the twenty-five and a half years after my daughter's birth. No prior concerns seemed important now; I wanted to meet my daughter.

Marcia told me my daughter's name was Lori, and she was a school social worker in Kansas City. She asked if I wanted to meet her. Of course, I replied that I did.

She said Lori had one question she would like for me to answer. I told her I was as ready now to answer it as I would ever be, expecting, "Why did you give me up?"

She told me Lori just wanted to know, "Where did I get all of this hair?" She explained Lori had gorgeous blond hair down to the middle of her back that was so curly and thick she couldn't at times get a comb through it.

I replied if she could see me, she would understand. I also told her I had some nieces with hair even thicker and curlier than mine.

Marcia continued, "You sound like such a wonderful person. Lori will be thrilled!"

The tears started flowing again.

As soon as I finished talking to Marcia, I called my mom, but I wasn't able to talk when she answered. Instead, I cried.

After realizing I was scaring Mom by crying, I told her everything Marcia had told me. She was thrilled and wanted to know when she could meet her.

Next, I called my sister Evelyn at work. I started crying as soon as I heard her voice. I managed to tell her everything. She cried and made plans to see me as soon as she got off work.

My friend Kathy was at work. When she answered the phone, I again started crying. She asked if someone had died. She told a co-worker I was crying and asked him to tell their boss an emergency had come up, and she had to leave.

The next person I tried to contact was my niece Norma, a licensed guidance counselor. She wasn't home, so I left a message for her to call.

Kathy arrived. We cried as I told her my news. She stayed with me until my sister arrived. Evelyn arrived with two bunches of pink carnations.

Lori called at 9 p.m.

"Sharon? This is Lori. I've known all of my life I was adopted and that I would try to find you when I turned 21. My dad died two years ago of cancer. I loved him very much and didn't try to find you while he was sick. When I was a child, I would always pretend I knew you and that you were a great person. I have a lot of love and respect for you. Because of your giving me up, I've had a great life and the best parents anyone could ever want. Even if you would have handpicked them, I couldn't have had better parents. I don't hold any grudge against you for giving me up. I know it must have been a difficult decision for you."

I thought, *What a wonderful answer to that prayer I had prayed so many years before.*

Lori asked about each family member listed on the adoption papers. Going down the list, I told her about each one. Filling me in on some of the details about how she found me, she told me her mom had handed her an envelope a few months earlier saying, "Here's what you've always wanted." Inside were the adoption papers with my name on them. She requested her original birth certificate from the State of Kansas and received it in three weeks. The adoption papers, not the original birth certificate, had all the important information she needed to contact me.

Once she knew my name and that I lived in Springfield, she called Stephanie, a friend from college who also lived in Springfield and asked if there were any Fiekers listed in the telephone book. As Stephanie started naming them, Lori got excited when my name was the last one listed and said, "Oh, that's her! She's still there."

While on Christmas vacation from work, Lori stayed with Stephanie for a few days. After Stephanie left for work, Lori drove by my house. My mailbox had some mail in it. She parked down the street, hoping to get a glimpse of me when I opened my door and reached for the mail. When the dogs next door started barking, she was afraid someone would call the police so she left. Returning a little later, she noticed the mail was gone, so she knew I was home. Knowing it wouldn't be good to approach my door on her own, she left.

Continuing, Lori told me she had my home address and telephone number, but she didn't know where I worked. She asked Stephanie's boyfriend to call me pretending to be an insurance agent with a price quote for my car insurance, hoping I would readily give him additional information. She thought she could possibly then be able to see me at work without my being aware of her presence. After learning of the reason for the call, I thanked him, told him I already had insurance, and hung up.

When that idea didn't work, Lori couldn't wait any longer to meet me. She returned home and asked her supervisor to call me.

After Lori's call that night, my niece Norma called to say she had been trying to call me since she got home from work, but my line was busy. She even called my brother John to see if anyone in the family had died. She told him about the message I had left on her machine. She thought my voice sounded different. Knowing I'm not one to talk on the phone, she couldn't imagine what was going on.

I told her I had good news, but I couldn't tell her without crying. She thought I might be getting married.

In hearing about Lori, she seemed more thrilled than I had ever known her to be about anything. After we hung up, she called John again.

John then called me. He hadn't known anything about my pregnancy in 1969, but Norma had told him about it a few years before this phone call. He told me, "Sharon, I think God was just waiting until He thought you could handle it."

I agreed.

Linda was the next person on my list to call. She had been a good friend for about twenty-three years. I asked if she could go to lunch. She told me she and Jim were taking off work at noon and going to St. Louis. She asked if we could have lunch the next week.

I started crying.

She then told me we could have lunch today. She tried to find out what was wrong, but I couldn't stop crying to tell her. She called her husband to explain she wanted to delay their trip. He told her to go to lunch with me because he had never known me to cry so something must be wrong.

As I began telling Linda my news over lunch, we started crying. She came over to my side of the booth and hugged me. About ten minutes later, she looked around the restaurant and said she should probably get back on her side since we were starting to attract attention.

Although Linda was hurt that I never felt I could tell her about my daughter, she was thrilled to hear the news. Her husband was happy for me, but he was afraid that I'd be hurt. Linda's daughter told her I had always been special to her, but she always noticed sadness about me. She never knew why she felt that sadness until she heard about Lori. Then, it all made sense.

I couldn't wait to find out more about Lori's life and to see her. What I had hoped for was becoming a reality.

children are a reward

Sons are a heritage from the LORD,
Children a reward from him.
(Psalm 127:3, NIV).

*L*ori called on Friday night to tell me she wanted to see me, and I told her I wanted to see her, too. Since one of my hobbies was photography, I added that I wanted to see every picture that had ever been made of her. She told me that wasn't any problem because her hobby was photography.

When my niece Kayleen arrived at Evelyn's house that same night, she knew something was different. Her mom seemed to be bursting with some news, so Kayleen asked her what was going on.

"Call Sharon," Evelyn insisted.

"Sharon, what's going on? I've never in my life seen my mother look so happy. She's just glowing," Kayleen said.

I told her about Lori, and she admitted Norma had told her I had been pregnant. After we cried together, she thought it was the best news ever, and she could understand the effect on her mom.

I called my niece Cathy, whom Norma had also told a few years earlier about my pregnancy. I never knew Norma had told so many people. Norma's answer was that it had come up as a discussion of how family secrets cause low self-esteem and unresolved grief.

On Saturday, Mom and I visited my brother Ron and his family to tell them my news. At first, I told them they would need to get the Kleenexes. As soon as I began telling about Lori, my niece Cindy said, "Pass the Kleenexes." They were overwhelmed with joy and happiness.

On Sunday, I arrived for church a little early, and I told some of my friends about Lori. Soon, my whole class was wondering why we were crying, so I told them my secret. For someone who'd kept her feelings under a shell of protection for so many years, I opened up that week. Not one person expressed the disrespect I had dreaded.

My sister Edith called with excitement Sunday afternoon to tell me she had shared my news with her whole church. She hoped I didn't mind. I told her I didn't, and I had done the same thing at my church.

Fearing she might change her mind, I called Lori on Monday night and learned she was coming the following weekend. We agreed nine o'clock on Saturday morning would be a good time for her to arrive at my house. We would then plan on going to Mom's whenever we were ready.

I called Ron to tell him about Saturday. His wife Sheila told me Ron had shared my story in church on Sunday, and they hoped I didn't mind. I told her I didn't and that Edith and I had done the same thing at our churches. We agreed a beautiful story should be shared.

The telephone was my companion for the biggest part of the week. On Tuesday night, I told my coworkers about Lori. They were understanding and excited. By the next night, I had expected everyone in the building to know my story since gossip usually spreads like wildfire. A few months later, I mentioned my daughter to a coworker who hadn't heard anything about her. His reply:

"Sharon, do you know why so many people still don't know about her? Your story is the truth, not a rumor. Everyone has so much respect for you that to repeat it would cause them to feel they're gossiping about you. Hearing it from you and seeing your face glow makes it worthwhile to only hear it from you."

That next week I received many cards from friends and family. One card I received from a coworker had a turtle on the front that was coming out of its shell. She wrote a personal note:

> Sharon, I've watched a change in you for about the last two years. You've always been a special person, but there is a peace and contentment about you now that's a pleasure to watch. You will be a wonderful mother and friend to Lori. Remember I'm there if you need me. Connie Vaughan

I was overwhelmed with the love and support I received from my family and friends.

That next week, my niece Cindy sent me a letter. She had been quiet the day I had told her about Lori. Since she had never been told about my pregnancy when she was younger, my news was a total surprise.

> Dear Sharon, I've been thinking about you all evening, and I wanted to tell you some things. First off, I love you very much and think you are one of the most wonderful people I know. When I was a little girl, I remember that I always wanted to be around you. I loved spending nights with you, going shopping, seeing Santa, the fair, everything! I always thought you would make the neatest mom. When Mom &

Dad put you down as the guardian for my brother and me if something were to happen to them, I remember thinking we were so lucky. If something happened, we wouldn't have been alone, we would have had you. When Grandma would call me "Little Sharon" or when people would think you were my mom, I was always flattered. Remember when the nurse asked if you were the grandma? When I was in the hospital with the girls, I would call and you'd be right there. It meant a lot that you were there when we dedicated the girls. Sharon, when I learned you'd accepted Christ as your Savior, I was thrilled! As a little girl, I would pray for you to be saved.

Today when you were telling me about Lori, all of these thoughts floated around in my heart. She may have wonderful parents, but the lady who gave birth to her is pretty wonderful too! Lori is pretty lucky to be able to have you in her life. I'm so happy for you. I'm sure it will all turn out fine. Sharon, you and Lori are both in my prayers, and I will be around for you, too. Love, Cindy

When I read her letter, I cried. With all of the attention I received, I felt guilty and wonderful at the same time. Throughout the years, I had never felt I was deserving of any happiness. I was now happier than I ever thought possible. How would I be able to wait until the weekend when I could see my daughter for the first time face-to-face?

February 11, 1995 was the coldest day of the year outside with the temperatures being close to zero. Who could be concerned about the weather? I felt warm inside.

Lori arrived promptly at nine. Although Marcia had described her, I hadn't contemplated her beauty. Upon seeing her for the first time, I said, "Oh, you are beautiful!"

"You are, too!"

We hugged.

Finding out just how much we are alike was fascinating. Lori loved music although she said she couldn't sing. She brought photo albums just as I had requested. I had expected to see pictures of her, but most were of concerts she had attended. She had seen country music singers Brooks & Dunn in four states. She spent nearly every summer weekend at some music concert. I showed her my albums of the concerts I had attended. I saw the Righteous Brothers in Washington, D.C.; Elvis in three cities; Tom Jones in two cities; Neil Diamond twice; Tina Turner; Alabama; and others.

An eerie feeling surfaced when Lori got her small albums out and lined them in an orderly fashion on my coffee table and said, "I'm an organized person."

I can't count the times I had been told, "You're such an organized person." Most of her pictures of herself were judged by her as being good or bad based upon whether it was a good-hair day or a bad-hair day. I understood.

Lori told me about her friends who were all important to her. Since her present boyfriend David sounded different than her previous boyfriends she told me about, I asked, "Could he be 'the one'?"

"I'm not sure, but he's more special than any of the other guys I've dated."

Lori shared a lot about her friends, even intimate details. I thought, *Wow, this is just what a mother and daughter should talk about.*

The love Lori felt for her parents was obvious when she showed me their pictures along with the newspaper clipping about her dad's death. When she mentioned her brother, I remarked, "I remember being told when you were born that a lovely couple had been found who had adopted a baby boy two years earlier."

"Yes, that same information was written in the adoption papers," she said. "In reading the follow-up work by the social worker, I was amused to learn my brother had been a little jealous and had pinched me on one occasion."

The fact that Lori brought me a copy of the adoption papers meant a lot. Throughout the weekend, Lori was considerate of my feelings. She never once said anything to indicate she held a grudge against me.

Lori brought her thesis she completed while working on her master's degree in social work. In reading her reflection on her life, I didn't notice any indication of her ever having feelings of rejection. She had a beautiful childhood, and I appreciated her letting me read about it. Her parents obviously did a wonderful job in raising her. Reading something of hers that was so personal was an honor. Usually, the teachers grading them are the only ones fortunate enough to read a masterpiece of one's life.

The fact I was attending college impressed Lori, although she didn't understand how I could work full-time and attend classes. So much had been on my mind besides studying, especially since her phone call, I had thought about dropping out of school that semester.

Lori said, "Now let's have a role reversal. I'll say, 'Sharon, you can't drop out now. I'll be so proud of you to get your degree.'"

How could I think about dropping out after that?

Around three o'clock that afternoon, Lori and I drove by Stephanie's apartment to pick up her friend Jeanna who had come with her from Kansas City. We mentioned to Jeanna how we didn't see any resemblance in our appearance. Shocked, she replied, "You're serious? I can't believe you can't see it."

The three of us arrived at Mom's where thirty family members were waiting. Cameras flashed, and the video camera recorded.

Lori was fascinated to meet her cousins, especially those who had hair as curly as hers.

Ron teasingly asked, "Lori, are you late because Sharon introduced you to all of the turtles in her collection?"

Lori smiled, and I said, "I've already asked her. She doesn't collect turtles."

Just before I left Lori and Jeanna at Stephanie's apartment, I asked, "Would you like to go to church with me tomorrow morning?"

One of my friends at church said, "You two look so much alike, but more like sisters than mother and daughter." Being told how much we looked alike was exciting.

The saddest part of the weekend came as Lori and Jeanna prepared to leave. Lori hugged me and said, "My image of you came true. You are a great person." Then, she added, "Now you're not going to cry after I leave, are you?"

Although the tears would be different now, I knew I would cry many more.

Watching the two of them back from my driveway saddened me. How could I be depressed when I had just experienced the most wonderful weekend in my life?

Although I was deliriously happy one moment, I wondered if I would see Lori again. Would her curiosity be satisfied now that she had met me? Would she desire to see me again? Then, I would think about how wonderful and beautiful she was, and I was up in the clouds. Just as fast, back down again I'd go. These up-and-down emotions are appropriately known as the roller-coaster ride of reunions. I thought, *Well, Sharon, jump onboard for the beginning of the ride of your life.*

making a plan for my child

...and she became pregnant and gave birth to a son. When
she saw that he was a fine child, she hid him for three
months. But when she could hide him no longer, she got
a papyrus basket for him and coated it with tar and pitch.
Then she placed the child in it and put it among the reeds
along the bank of the Nile.
(Exodus 2:2,3, NIV)

*I*n reflecting over my weekend with Lori, I realized we spent a
lot of time talking about medical history. I was overwhelmed
with the similarities in our lives. At times, I thought, *Wow.
She is just like me.*

In a compassionate gesture, Lori had placed her hand on my
knee, saying, "I have some questions to ask that might be too
painful for you to answer. If so, I understand. You don't have to
answer them, but I would like to know a little about my birth

father. I know his physical size and hair color from the adoption papers."

I thought, *Why should he delight in a reunion with her when he'd chosen to ignore her after I had told him I was pregnant?* Then I thought, *Those feelings are probably the same her mom had when she learned Lori wanted to meet me.* So I replied, "I'll tell you everything I can. I think you have a right to know. Discussing him with you is not too painful for me."

Forgiveness goes a long way in making life better. Having learned to accept and offer forgiveness, I knew I had to forgive Lori's birth father. I said, "I don't object to your finding him. His name is Bob, and I'll help in any way I can, but I don't care to ever see him again. Since I had anticipated your concern, I tried to find him this past week, but his name is too common. I can't remember his middle name, although I know his date of birth. Too many years have passed, and I don't have any pictures of him nor do I see any resemblance of him in you. My sister Evelyn has some old home movies of us at a party, and we can go through them. He might not remember me or the night I told him I was pregnant. I'm sorry for not being more helpful."

"That's okay. He's not really that important anyway."

Knowing Lori had said this for my benefit although her medical history was important to her, I said, "I'll continue to try to find him."

Lori wanted to know everything she could about my life with Bob. I told her that I met him when I was living in St. Louis with my sister Evelyn and her husband Gary. They had introduced me to their friends, Pam and Perry, as well as Beth and Benjamin. I spent time with them and their children. I loved spending time with my niece Kayleen and her friends. Beth and Benjamin introduced me to their great-nephew Bob who moved to St. Louis after serving in the Marines. Bob and I spent our first date at a Cardinal's baseball game. We both loved to dance and went to nightclubs nearly every time we went out, or we would drink at his apartment. I considered myself a social drinker although I wasn't legally old enough to drink. Bob turned twenty-two during the time we dated; I was twenty.

Although we didn't date on a steadily basis, we dated during a period of about six months. Sex became a part of our relationship although neither of us used any birth control. Neither Evelyn nor Gary cared for Bob. On one occasion, Gary offered to take me to Bob's apartment since he had seen him with another girl. I didn't want to believe he'd be with anyone else, but I wouldn't go see for myself. Too afraid to face the truth, I preferred to ignore it.

After Evelyn and Gary made plans to move to Washington state, I rented an apartment. Once I realized I was pregnant, I didn't know where to turn. Hoping that everything would turn out "happily ever after" for me, I told Bob I was pregnant. I haven't seen him since that night. Reality hit fast when I realized he didn't love me or care what I did about "my problem." He offered no suggestions or assistance. I cried myself to sleep that night and many nights thereafter. Being pregnant, unmarried, scared, abandoned, ashamed, alone, and knowing I would have to quit my job, how would I get by? What was I going to do? How would I ever tell Mom and Dad?

Although I had friends and coworkers, I felt I had nowhere to turn. I kept everything to myself. I was not aware of any pregnancy care centers to ask for assistance. My friends would have been willing to help if I would have confided in them. I had too much pride to admit I needed help.

Having always loved children, I also had always thought they deserved both a loving mother and father. Since getting married and raising our baby together was out of the question, I knew I had only one choice: to make a plan of adoption for my baby. Instead of the life I had to offer with the stigma of being illegitimate, I wanted my baby to have a better life with loving parents. An unmarried girl with a child in the '60s was socially unacceptable.

Why did I feel so quick to relieve Bob of any responsibility in making that decision? Could it have been because he was so quick to tell me he didn't care, and it was my problem? Why did I accept full blame for having sex outside of marriage, getting pregnant, and making such a decision for our baby alone? Why was providing for our child more my responsibility than his? Those questions remain prevalent with many young people today, over thirty-five years later.

My parents lived only about four hours away. The longest trip of my life was driving home to tell them I was pregnant and that I planned to place my baby for adoption. How would they feel? Would they disown me? Would they be relieved? Although they would have allowed me to stay at home and parent my baby, they agreed adoption was the best answer. We lived in an era then where wondering what the neighbors might think was common. I didn't think it would be fair to expect my mom to help me since my three youngest brothers were still at home. Having my child raised like a sibling wasn't an option for me.

Mom called my sister-in-law Marlene. She and my oldest brother Charles said I could live with them in Kansas City until after my baby's birth. Bob's great-aunt Beth told me I could spend my last two weeks in St. Louis with her and Benjamin and their three children. I shared a bedroom with their two daughters; the youngest one had beautiful long blond hair that hung in ringlets. Bob had previously gone to their house every few days, but he stayed away while I was there.

Although I didn't confide in Beth or anyone else, I felt that she knew I was pregnant. I was in a state of denial. My pregnancy wasn't actually noticeable because of my large frame, so I was never asked about being pregnant. Since oversized clothing like sack dresses and tunics were in, I never wore maternity clothes.

I moved home with Mom and Dad for a short time before going to Kansas City. Norma told me that she, her mother, and her brother came to get me. She and her mother drove home in their car, and her brother rode with me in my car. She said we left after dark to go home, although I have no recollection of it. She remembered thinking it was weird we were leaving at night, but she later wondered if we left so maybe the neighbors wouldn't notice.

Until I got to Kansas City, I didn't receive any prenatal care. Marlene made an appointment for me with her doctor who took care of the adoption arrangements. My baby daughter was born in August 1969. I didn't see her nor did I protest the recommendation that I not see her. Signs were placed on my door on both sides to ensure I didn't leave my room and that my baby wasn't brought to me.

Hours after my daughter's birth, I started hemorrhaging and nearly died. Because of the times, the complications, and possibly the fact I was placing a baby for adoption, I was heavily medicated during my six-day stay. My baby was born early that morning so Marlene went home soon afterward to get some rest. Coming back into my room and learning I had almost died, she was upset with the hospital staff. She had left her telephone number with them to be called in case of an emergency. Letting such a mistake slide without letting them know her true feelings wasn't an option for Marlene. That incident was one of the few things I remembered about being in the hospital. Norma told me her mom had shared with her that the nurses ignored me because of their unwed-mother bias. During my first two days in the hospital, I received a transfusion of two pints of blood.

My nephew Duane was twelve-years-old at the time, and Norma was nine. She remembers getting excited thinking about me with a baby and asking her mother, "What did Sharon have?"

Marlene told her, "I don't know. Sharon won't be bringing her baby home. Don't ask her about it when she comes home because it will make her sad to talk about it." Norma later made up for all of that silence.

The only counseling I received from the social worker at the hospital was, "Going on with your life and forgetting about this part of it would be the best thing for you." However, she didn't offer instructions on how to do that. Other than my immediate family, I told one friend Kathy about my daughter. Although she attempted at times to discuss my daughter over the years, I would usually quickly change the subject.

Feeling I deserved happiness, forgiveness, or to be in church after my experience wasn't an option for me. Being a birth mom did a major number on my self-esteem. Believing that I deserved only one chance at happiness, I felt I had already blown that opportunity. Although I knew I had made the right decision for my daughter, I couldn't get over the guilt.

My life started looking up in 1972. After buying a new vehicle and noticing a few minor problems the first week, I called my salesman and was advised to bring my vehicle in. Another salesman named Ryan met me to assist with the problem. Later, I learned Ryan had asked my salesman, "Who's the girl with the hair? I've got to meet her." My hair was thick and down to my waist. I wrapped it on large curlers the size of juice cans to straighten it. My first impression of Ryan was one of arrogance; however, I agreed to go out with him. I changed my opinion of him soon after that and continued to date him.

Although I learned Ryan was a divorced father of two children who had been adopted at birth, I didn't tell him about my daughter. On one occasion, he took me out of town to meet his parents. He was seven years older than me, and he treated me like a queen. He seemed fascinated with my long hair and seemed to enjoy the attention we got because of it. He'd always make a big deal of lifting my long hair from inside my coat to ensure it hung down along the outside.

Ryan and I had been seeing each other about twice a week for about six months. Then all of a sudden, I stopped hearing from him. I called him and found out he was going back to his ex-wife, a devastating revelation for me. He hadn't known how to tell me, so he just didn't call. Later, I learned from his best friend that his ex-wife had threatened to move out of state with their children if he didn't take her back. When I finally talked to Ryan in person a week later, I asked him, "Can you look me in the eyes and tell me you love her and not me?"

"No, I can't do that," he replied.

Deep down, I knew I couldn't interfere or prevent his children from having their parents together again. After crying for days, I buried my grief once again.

Using an acronym of a Turtle's Shell, I'll describe my then perception of myself under that shell of protection:

T*ARNISHED*	S*AD*
U*NWORTHY*	H*IDDEN*
R*EJECTED*	E*MOTIONS*
T*ROUBLED*	L*OVELESS*
L*ONELY*	L*OST*
E*MPTY*	
S*CARED*	

Those words weren't a side of me I would let others see. Years later after watching one of my presentations, a friend said, "I missed an 's' when I saw that acronym. I thought it spelled, "Turtle's Hell." Losing at love twice, I vowed never again to let anyone get close enough to me to hurt me.

Ryan continued calling me, and we would go out occasionally although he remarried his ex-wife. My friends hated the way I allowed him to control my life. I would go out dancing and meeting men, but I wouldn't let anyone get close to my heart. No one else measured up to Ryan. I would compare the actions of anyone new to him. I loved to dance, probably because I would still be close physically without mentally having to reveal those feelings locked inside. On the inside, however, I knew I was wasting my time. No one could ever make me forget Ryan. He seemed to have a knack for knowing when I wasn't thinking about him. Just when I would begin to think of someone new, he would call. Telling him not to contact me at all was difficult, but I knew I had to do it. My friends were pleased when I told them I had told Ryan not to call me.

Believing I could have been in love with him without telling him about the most important part of my past is difficult for me to comprehend. You would think I could have trusted him, knowing he had adopted his children at their birth. I wonder if I would have told him about my daughter if we had eventually married.

I realize now that Ryan's ending our relationship wouldn't have been so devastating had the experience with Bob and placing my daughter for adoption not occurred. So much unresolved grief was involved before meeting Ryan, what was a little more to be added to grief already buried deep?

shell of protection

As for God, his way is perfect; the word of the LORD is
flawless. He is a shield for all who take refuge in him.
(2 Samuel 22:31, NIV)

*I*n February 1974, I needed something to help me get over
my bad experiences with love. A new job seemed to be a
way to start. I began looking for an apartment so I could
live without a roommate. The weekend before I changed jobs, I got
my long, thick, down-to-my-waist hair cut to shoulder length to
provide a new look.

On February 11, 1974, I started working as a clerk stenographer
at the local police department. Continuing to meet new friends and
coworkers was part of the change. But the story about my daughter
remained a secret from all of them. I met my next-door neighbor
Dodie, who was the type of neighbor everyone should have. Her
husband died a few years after I met her. She never had children,
and she treated me like the daughter she never had. She didn't drive.

I took her to her doctors' appointments when I could. When I was having a bad day at work, I stopped by her apartment. Soon, I would be laughing and forgetting whatever had been bothering me. As close as we were, I regret never having told her about my daughter.

On holidays, I enjoyed spending time with my nieces and nephews when they would visit my parents. My nieces would occasionally spend the night at my apartment. Often, I was told, "You would make a wonderful mother."

I would always think, *If you only knew.*

In 1985, my friend Kathy and I bought a .35 mm. camera and signed up for some fun college classes to learn about photography. We began to think about working toward a college degree.

My third-grade teacher had planted a seed in my mind to go to college. Although I no longer wanted to become a teacher, my dream of earning a degree was becoming a reality. Dodie often asked about my classes and offered to help me study. Whenever I had some stress relating to my job or too much homework, she would often say she was proud of me for working toward that degree. My favorite classes were psychology, sociology, and criminal justice. I enjoyed writing term papers after researching a subject. Although not an intentional result of my college classes, I found out about myself from studying the behaviors of others.

Over the years, I had a few special relationships. In 1990, I met Raymond. Although he didn't become my knight in shining armor, he did become a good friend. We would go out to eat, go to movies, or stay home and watch television. My former boyfriend Ryan called from out of the blue after 18 years. Hadn't he always seemed to know whenever I showed a little more than the usual interest in someone?

He said, "I'm separated from my wife. I would like to see you."

I felt instead that his wife probably had gone out of town for the weekend without him. Still, I agreed to see him.

Television talk shows had started doing reunion stories, and I was all caught up in "what if" concerning Ryan. My coworkers thought the fact he had called after 18 years was exciting. After he picked me up, we went out for a drink. With a surprised, disgusted look after he reached for a cigarette, I asked, "Do you smoke?"

"Yes, I always have."

"I don't remember that." Of course, I had only remembered the good things. After I got home that night, I got out some pictures of us when we first started dating. Sure enough, he was holding a cigarette in each picture. I looked at those pictures and wondered, *Why did I pine after him for so many years?*

While we were talking that same night, I asked him, "Do you have any idea how much you hurt me?"

"Yes, I know. I'm not proud of it, but you weren't the only one who was hurt. I also suffered."

The timing was right for him to enter my life again so I could place that part of my life into perspective. Getting all of that pent-up hurt and frustration out in the open helped me to move on. We never dated again.

In one of my college classes, the professor divided the class into groups to complete and discuss our own self-esteem inventory. We were to rate ourselves from one to ten, with ten being the best. My self-rating was a three. An attractive lady was in my group, and she couldn't understand why I had rated myself so low.

Over the years, I felt inferior, inside and out. Although I had been told I had pretty hair, beautiful eyes, and a nice smile, I felt those were the extent of my good qualities. I couldn't imagine any beauty about the rest of me. So much worth had been placed by me on my outward appearance and my inner secrets that I failed to see anything positive. During class that night, I got teary-eyed just thinking about how I felt completely unworthy of praise and affection. Diverting the subject to keep the tears from flowing, I told my classmates, "I can't talk about my low self-rating."

During that same period, I watched a movie about an adoptee who was dying and needed a bone marrow transplant to survive. The birth mother was found, and the transplant was done. *Lifeline, The Action Guide to Adoption Search* by Virgil L. Klunder was given as a source for finding a lost loved one. Until then, I had always felt I didn't deserve to intrude in my daughter's life. The possibility she might need me had never entered my mind, and it changed everything. I ordered the book.

After reading that book, I called Norma to see if she knew the name of the hospital where my daughter was born. I had been successful in blocking out of my mind many things, including the name of the hospital. Norma didn't remember, but she called her mother and told her I was asking about my daughter's birth. Learning my daughter was born just over the line in Kansas instead of Missouri was a relief. From the book, I learned she could obtain her original birth certificate because of the open adoption laws in Kansas. Because I had never married and still lived in the same general area, I knew she could easily find me when and if she chose to do so. Although I had hoped she would find me, I still didn't feel at that time that I deserved to meet her.

Because Norma had a master's degree in guidance and counseling, she tried to get me to talk more about my daughter's birth. But I still didn't want to talk about it with her or anyone else. I had always felt that I made the right decision for my daughter, and I wanted to leave it at that.

Although I was a good person, a law-abiding citizen, I also knew I wasn't living according to God's law. I hadn't attended church since I moved out on my own. During summer 1993, I had wondered why I felt so unhappy. I had a good job, many good friends, and a loving family. Some of my good friends started retiring from their jobs, and I started thinking about how lonely life would be without my job. For nineteen years, I had put my all into my job, and it had become my life. To me, my job seemed to be the only area of my life where I could claim success. Having witnessed the changes occurring in my friends after they retired, I knew I had to get a life outside of my work.

Wondering about things that were missing in my life got me to thinking about God. Could He be the missing link? Occasionally, I would still get together with my friend Raymond. We would often discuss God, going to church, and that part of our lives that had been so important to both of us. We had similar childhoods, both being raised in Christian homes with Christian values. Remembering my friends from church while growing up, I began to miss that special fellowship.

In July 1993, I made a list of churches and planned to attend a different one every Sunday until I found one I liked. When the Men's Quartet sung during a 4th of July service at the first church on my list, I thought, *Wow! They sure can sing*! While reading the church's motto, "Where No One Stands Alone," I remembered the copy of the song taped in my Bible. I knew this church was the one for me. After going to the singles class, I met several people who became good friends.

Later, that same month, I woke up from my sleep crying in the middle of the night, and I started praying. Realizing Jesus Christ was part of what was missing in my life, I asked Him to be my personal Savior. For many years, I had thought I could never be forgiven for all my sins leading up to placing my daughter for adoption and that I just couldn't be worthy of His love. How could I have been so wrong? Had I opened up and shared those negative feelings with someone, my life might have been different. However, I believe that everything happens for a reason. I also believe that God had a plan for my life, and He was just waiting for the right time to show me.

On the next Mother's Day, the pastor recognized the mothers by asking them to stand. I sat in my seat and thought, *I'm a mother, but I can't stand. No one will respect me if they know the truth about me—that I'd given up my baby girl for adoption.* Although I had felt like a new person, I hadn't yet forgiven myself. I had started opening up a little with my friends, but I still couldn't reveal the real me.

In 1994, my neighbor and friend Dodie died at the age of eighty-six. Another friend died about a week later. He was Officer Bob. The last week prior to his death, he had come by my desk and told a coworker, "Connie, you know that Sharon Fieker has the most beautiful smile of anyone I know. I have to come by her desk when I get to work every night to see her smile. It's like a jump-start to get me started on my shift."

He then turned around, looked at me, smiled, and said, "Oh, Sharon, I didn't know you were there." His statement was the nicest thing anyone had ever said about my smile.

Bryan Cummins had not yet met me at the time he wrote this poem. Even if he had known me, he could not have written a better description of my self-perception all of those years inside that protective shell:

The Man Behind the Smile

I find at times I must wear this smile
So no one will ask me why
Eyes filled with joy, but all the while
Tears of pain run deep inside

Look past the shield of laughter
To find the vulnerable spot behind
You must first turn back the book's cover
To learn the knowledge that is inside
A veil of blue to hide the gray
You must look hard to see
A disguise of happiness to hide the pain
A mirage in the desert sea
Believe the lie of joyful bliss
Remain in your denial
But you must look deeper if you wish
To see the man behind the smile.

©1998 Bryan Cummins

Two weeks after the deaths of my friends, I attended a singles retreat with my Sunday school class. The timing of the retreat was appropriate, and it was led by Dr. Jim Towns from Nacogdoches, Texas. He helped me more than he'll ever know. Grief was the topic of one of his lectures. Later, I read one of his books wherein he wrote:

> Reach out to people once again. After the loss of a spouse, the natural reaction is to withdraw and lead a secluded and reclusive lifestyle. After a legitimate healing time, seclusion becomes unhealthy. People need people to maintain sanity and emotional health. If you are to recover completely, you simply must reach out in love to people once again. At first, you may be able to reach out only a little bit. But regardless of how raw or burned your feelings are and how frightening and painful the experience may be—you must continue to reach out. Remember that there can be no new life without the accompanying element of risk. (67)[1]

This advice was what I needed to hear. Although it was offered for those grieving the death of a spouse, it is good advice for grieving any loss or going through a rough time. Could it help me finally come to terms with grieving for my daughter?

spiritual awareness

"For I know the plans I have for you," declares the
LORD, "plans to prosper you and not to harm
you, plans to give you hope and a future."
(Jeremiah 29:11, NIV)

During the fall semester 1994, I enrolled in a Death &
Dying class. The students bonded as we went inside
our inner feelings and wound up crying nearly every
week. I prepared a written and oral presentation of "The Shell
Within." I chose a turtle from my collection to use as a prop on
the night of my final. After my teacher read my paper, she told me
she had intended to bring a turtle that night. I didn't know then
just how much of that shell I would eventually reveal.

I used the analogy of the actions of a turtle to explain unresolved grief: "When a turtle approaches danger, it goes into its
shell and stays until the danger is over. Each step forward for the
turtle is a risk, but it moves forward slowly. Each step forward to

resolve our grief may seem like a risk, but we must take it. To stay withdrawn is not healthy."

I quoted Ann Kaiser Stearns:

> One of the ways that scars remain is that our view of the world is colored by past experience. Vows made to ourselves years ago such as "I'll never let myself get hurt again," continue to dominate aspects of our lives. By completely closing down the gates between ourselves and further injury, we also close down the channels through which could flow what is needed for our nourishment. (132)[2]

A glance of my life was revealed in that paper. Demonstrating how I had gone through some of the stages of grief, I wrote about the breakup of a romance with Ryan, my former boyfriend. Although I met new friends, I found it easier to build a wall of protection around myself rather than risk being hurt again. Being stuck in the stage of resolving the grief was included in that paper along with seeing Ryan after eighteen years and expressing my feelings toward him.

During those eighteen years, I hadn't realized that Ryan wasn't totally responsible for all that happened. Some of that responsibility fell on my shoulders. Because I had reacted in that way, I blamed him for ruining my life. A similar reaction was obvious in the way I buried the grief of placing my daughter for adoption, but I didn't mention that story in that paper.

Preventing others from being aware of my pain was a way I coped. Blaming others is easier than delving into the real problem. Blaming Bob, Lori's birth father, for almost twenty-five years for ruining my life was my way of coping. Neither Ryan nor Bob forced me to react the way I did. God gave me the strength and wisdom to learn to forgive myself, Bob, and Ryan. Learning to forgive others just as we have been forgiven goes a long way in mending hurts. If I would have truly learned that lesson years ago, my life would have been different. Would I have blamed either Bob or Ryan for ruining my life had we married and later divorced? My relationships suffered because I wasn't honest with my feelings, and I didn't deal with the deep-rooted pain. I believe now that everything happens for a reason and I know the past is something I cannot change, so I try to learn from it.

In that same paper, I wrote about how Mom dealt with grief. I discussed grief with her and wrote about it. After my father's death, an aunt told me, "Be sure to keep an eye on your mom since she is good about hiding her feelings." Sound familiar? Like mother, like daughter? Mom kept a lot of her feelings to herself when her first-born son, J.C., was killed at the age of fourteen years during a tornado in the early forties. His pictures were never displayed around our house like those of the rest of us.

A few years before I wrote that paper, my brother Ron moved into the vicinity where J.C. had been buried. He noticed someone else had already placed some flowers on the grave on Memorial Day. The same thing happened the next year. A woman came to him at the cemetery the next year as he was placing flowers on the grave. She introduced herself as Helen. She had been J.C.'s girl-friend prior to his death while they had been in school. Helen had been placing flowers on his grave every year since his death. She married and had children and grandchildren, but she never missed placing flowers on J.C.'s grave every Memorial Day. My mom later called Helen, and they met one summer day in 1994. They were able to spend the day reminiscing. Helen asked Mom, "Do you remember my telling you on the day of his funeral, 'Your son will always have a warm place in my heart?'"

Mom remembered. Talking helped her work through her feel-ings. She got to talk about J.C. with someone who knew him then, and they shared pictures and memories.

I discussed J.C.'s death with Mom, and she said, "I never wanted to talk about his death all of those years because to talk about it always made me sad. Anyone around me would also get sad, so why bring it up?" For many years, she had hidden under a shell or wall of protection. Did I learn from her? After those discussions with her, she started displaying pictures of J.C. on the wall alongside pictures of the rest of the family.

"Oh, it just happened because of fate" is a phrase that I used to say. Many times, I started a story with, "You'll never believe what happened to me today." The response I usually received was, "Yes, concerning you, I'll believe it." Coming up with an appropriate acrostic for the fate issue, I like to explain circumstances happen because of my:

> **F**ather's
> **A**ctions
> **T**imely
> **E**xplained

I now believe events in my life happen for a reason, not because of a mere coincidence. I like the explanation found in my favorite verse, Jeremiah 29:11. By the time you finish this book, I pray you'll also realize that God has a plan for your life, just as He does mine.

Our prayers are always answered although not always as fast or in the same way we would like. We have to depend upon God's timing. Looking back, I can see how my going to a church service again in 1993 was at the appropriate time. God used the next two years to prepare me for an unexpected wonderful thing that was to come: The reunion with my daughter.

overabundance of love

May the Lord make your love increase and overflow for each
other and for everyone else, just as ours does for you.
(1 Thessalonians 3:12, NIV)

I took the film from our wonderful weekend to the one-hour
photo lab because I couldn't wait to get the prints back.
Lori did the same thing, and we sent each other reprints
along with a Valentine that crossed in the mail. Lori wrote:

> Thank you and your family for welcoming Jeanna and me
> into your hearts and homes. It's kind of funny how Marcia
> & many co-workers see so many resemblances whereas at
> first we didn't see any. Now I can see a few things such as our
> smiles. David sent a floral arrangement to me at work and
> roses when he picked me up. I'm starting to believe he's a
> keeper. I'll keep you informed. Love, Lori

My niece Kayleen wrote in the Valentine she sent me:

> Sharon, I wanted to write you to let you know how happy I was to meet Lori. She is a beautiful, intelligent, outgoing person whom I enjoyed meeting very much. I'm so proud of you and happy that you have been blessed with finally meeting your wonderful daughter. You can finally rest easier because a difficult chapter of your life is over—the not knowing where or what she was. Now the most wonderful chapter will begin—When the two of you will learn about each other and grow to love the beautiful people you each are.
>
> Sharon, I love you very much. You have always been special to me, as I stated in the letter I wrote to Lori. Other than my parents, I think you are the first person I have memories of. I just wanted to say Congratulations—and here's to a wonderful future! If you need anything, let me know. Love, Kayleen

My friends and family sent me meaningful Valentines and notes. Some family members wrote a letter to Lori at my request along with some pictures so she would have some way of remembering them. Lori appreciated this effort since they helped her learn more about them and me.

I sent a note along with the videotape from our first day together:

> Lori, I had forgotten how emotional I got at the beginning of the tape. Oh, well, I guess 25–1/2 years of buried guilt deserves a lot of emotion. Never in all of these years did I think I deserved such love and happiness as I received from you, my family, and my friends. During times like these, I've realized how much I've taken my family and friends for granted. It's been overwhelming to hear and know of so much love. They've been so supportive of me. For you to actually tell me that you didn't hold any grudge was more than I ever hoped to hear. Even though I told you, "No more tears," I have still shed a few.

Before Lori left my house that first time, I asked her if she thought it would be all right if I mailed a letter to her mom. She did. Here is part of what I wrote:

> Dear Marge, This is a difficult letter to write, but I feel I must express my gratitude to you for so many things. First of all, you were the answer to many of my prayers for raising Lori into the special person she is today. Second of all, thanks for giving Lori the copy of the adoption decree with my name on it. I know it wasn't an easy decision for you to make.
>
> We definitely have one thing in common: Our #1 concern has always been what's best for Lori.
>
> My life has been like an emotional roller-coaster ride from the minute Marcia made that first phone call to me. I started crying almost immediately, and it has been difficult to suddenly bring those feelings to surface without crying after burying them for over 25 years in Lori's best interest. You see, I had a hard time realizing I deserved ever learning how beautiful and wonderful a person she turned out to be.
>
> I can't express how happy I was to hear Lori tell me that she had the best parents and upbringing a child could ever wish for. Even if I would have handpicked you, I couldn't have found better parents. That was always what I wanted for her. It meant so much for her to tell me she didn't hold a grudge against me for giving her up; and because of my decision, she had you.
>
> I told Lori when she left Sunday that I wouldn't cry any more, but I wasn't exactly truthful. Well, rather than crying, they have been tears of joy. Nobody at work will tell the others about it like they usually do when there is something to spread: They all feel it is such a beautiful story that it just has to be told by me. I am getting better though at telling it without crying so much. Of course, thanks to your unselfishness, I now have pictures to go along with the beautiful story.

It is now easier to tell the story with a really big smile rather than tears.

Again, I will be eternally grateful to you for raising Lori with such high moral standards and the best upbringing anyone could ever want.

Thanks again for giving Lori the kind of life you did and for making it possible for me to meet her. I can never thank you enough for allowing this moment to happen. Love, Sharon

Soon, I learned that Lori was like me in yet another way: We both love to send cards. My birthday card from her mentioned that the best things in life come from nature. Lori's friend Jeanna sent me a letter after my birthday that meant more to me than words can express:

Sharon, I've been meaning to sit down and write this since we got back, but things have been pretty hectic lately for one reason or another. This is the first time I've had the opportunity to get to it. First of all, let me wish you a belated happy birthday. I hope you had as wonderful a day as I did. If you remember, I am a huge basketball fan, and I was lucky enough to get a ticket to the Big 8 Tournament for the weekend, so I was happy. Besides, Lori and some friends took me out to dinner and dancing afterwards. So to say the least, I had a great time.

Anyway, I wanted to tell you just how much I enjoyed meeting you, and what a wonderful family you have. As awkward as the situation could have been, you all made it an incredible experience. I have never been involved in anything quite like that, as I'm sure you can imagine. So, thank you for welcoming me as well as Lori. I know I can't even begin to contemplate the emotions and feelings you must have been having and probably still are, but you completely put those second and only showed concern for what Lori was feeling and dealing with, and that let me know immediately that you are a special person. Then, if I had any doubt, I only had to meet your family and see them with you. The way they talk about you and the way they are with you could leave no doubt in anyone's mind as to the kind of person you are.

That's why I've wanted to write to you. Not only to say thank you but I feel you can learn so much about a person from the people they interact with, and I might be able to let you know how I and a lot of other people feel about Lori. Let me say that I am so thankful for whatever took place in the past so that Lori and I had the opportunity to become friends. I completely believe that every event in our lives happens for a reason and by design, what we choose to do with those situations is up to us and is what makes us who we are. That's why I choose not to regret the things I have done in the past. I can't change them, and it's because of those choices that I'm the person I am. As long as I'm happy with who I am then my life is in order, and only good things can happen. That's why I know it was meant for Lori and me to cross paths, as it was meant for the two of you to find each other again. I can only guess at the countless times you have questioned yourself as to the choice you made 25 years ago, but please don't question it ever again. It is one of many things that made you and Lori the people you are today. Believe me, that is a good thing.

I met Lori only a few years ago, but she and I have developed a relationship that I can only compare to that of sisters. I was not fortunate enough to have a sister; but if I had, I can only hope that we would have been as close as Lori and me. Actually, it's probably better this way because we never had to go through the fights and arguments that siblings would. Anyway, Lori has to be the most understanding, kindest, and big-hearted person I know, not to mention one of the most intelligent people I've ever met. She has to be the best listener I know. I can be talking about something off the top of my head and I may not even think it's that important, but you can bet Lori will hear every word and remember the conversation long after it took place. She is a loyal person, and it takes a lot for her to ever believe that there isn't something worthwhile in everyone. On the other hand, you can bet if you lie to her or betray her trust you know it is next to impossible to ever regain it. These are not merely my observations and opinions, I have had many conversations with mutual friends of ours, and they have the same opinions. That's how I know she would never be anything but honest and up front with you or anybody else. It may take her awhile to voice her opinion for fear of hurting someone's feelings, but she would never compromise her beliefs just to keep from hurting them. She would just agonize how she could have made it easier for the other person for the next month.

I never had the opportunity to meet her Dad but I know her Mom, and she is a wonderful lady. I can't imagine how difficult this must have been for her, but I promise you she would never stand in the way of giving Lori whatever she needs or makes her happy. She is a reserved person, but her love for Lori and her brother is extremely apparent. I know Lori has told you about her, but I want you to know it's all true and not just the prejudices of a daughter. She is truly a strong, intelligent, and loving person. After meeting you, it is quite obvious that Lori is a lucky person, because whatever wonderful qualities were not inherited she had the opportunity to develop from one great lady. Not too many people in this world can say that.

You know, I was looking at the pictures we took while we were there, and it amazes me how much she looks like you. I've always told Lori she has the greatest smile and now I know where that comes from, along with the most beautiful head of hair I've ever seen. You two have identical smiles. I can be in a rotten mood and Lori can walk into the room with that smile on her face, and my mood instantly begins to improve. That smile can do nothing but brighten anybody's day. So, you just keep on smiling, and know that somewhere you made somebody's day better, I guarantee it. I don't know why Lori doesn't see some of the wonderful qualities she has, but I think she's figured out that I don't say these things just to be nice, they are really true. For some reason though, she has a hard time believing what a special and unique person she truly is. It is a rare thing in this world to find people who are as honest and have a genuine integrity as she does. She is one of those people that you never have a doubt in your mind as to what side of the line she will be on. You know what her values and morals are up front, and she doesn't compromise them to satisfy people or situations. And I think you probably know as well if not better than me how unbelievable that can be in this day and age.

I can honestly say that there was only one person in this world I looked up to as a role model and hoped I could be as good and caring as they were while I was growing up, and that was my mother. That is until I met Lori. She is the only other person I know who I actually look to as the type of person I strive to be. We are a lot alike in some ways but we can be totally opposite in a lot of other ways. Maybe that's why we're so close, who knows. I just hope I've been as supportive and attentive to her as she has been for me. She is as dear to me as any one in my family, and I only want the best for her.

Anyway, I don't know how well I've been able to express in words how I feel about Lori, but maybe I was able to give you some insight as to not only my feelings but how most people I know feel about Lori. I truly hope the two of you take the opportunity to get to know each other and somehow be a part of each other's lives. There is always enough room for more friends and love in everyone's life. You are both blessed to have so many friends and family who love and care about you, and I feel privileged to have Lori in my life and to have had the opportunity to be a part of meeting you and your family. Take care and know that you truly are a wonderful person who deserves only the best.

May all your hopes and dreams come true! Jeanna

After reading that letter, I got choked up, as did Evelyn and Mom after I read it to them over the phone. My friend Kathy said, "Sharon, I feel like I just got through reading a letter written about you. Do you remember telling me about what Officer Bob told Connie about your smile? The only changes that would need to be made for it to be a letter about you would be to change the name."

The fact that Jeanna took the time to write such a loving letter meant a lot to me. It said a lot for the type of person she is. I laminated that letter and the cards I received from Lori that first year because I showed them so many times they wore thin.

My brother John surprised me that week by sending a letter:

> Thanks for the pictures. The two of you look more like sisters than mother and daughter. I wish I could express my feelings more but I think you get the idea. Right? I bet the newness hasn't worn off yet. Thank God for the joy of life, and life for the joy of each other. Keep in touch, Sharon, and I'll try to keep writing. Sis, we love you!

A few days after my birthday, I mailed a letter to Lori:

> Even though I don't like to think about being another year older, I do love getting cards and being remembered by my friends and family. I got 27 cards in all. You and I are a lot alike since we sure have a lot of friends. Just as the picture in my hallway of the turtle with friends on its back reminds me, "I get by with a little help from my friends."

On Easter, Lori sent me a card along with a picture of her and David. A few weeks later, she sent me my first Mother's Day card:

> I'll bet you receive several Mother's Day cards this year from your family. I'm glad to have been able to allow you to grow as you tell me you've done since February. You are very deserving of happiness. I hope it continues to follow you wherever you go. Love, Lori

Mother's Day at my church this year was different than the previous year. When our pastor asked the mothers to stand and be recognized, I thought, *I am a mother.* With tears in my eyes and a big smile, I stood with the other mothers.

After church that day, I went to Mom's house to give her an 8x10 enlargement of the picture of her, Lori, and me. Evelyn gave me a red rose in a bud vase and a card with a note, "Sharon, Happy Mother's Day on your first of many to come. It took more love to do it your way, so now just enjoy! Love, Evelyn."

Evelyn, my mom, my sister Edith, and I drove to Kansas City that next weekend to see Lori and Jeanna. We met David while we were there, and I learned he was as neat as I had expected. Lori showed me one turtle in a shadow box of memorabilia in her bedroom that she had collected over the years. She had made it in Brownies or Girl Scouts. We all then drove to my sister Betty's to help her celebrate her birthday. We watched some of Evelyn's old home movies so Lori could see her birth father, Bob, on film. My memories of him had been of little help to her in describing him. Although it was a fast-moving home movie, she could see a little bit of what he and I were like then. She learned from whom she got her love of music and dancing, since we were dancing during most of it.

Lori said, "Sharon, Bob doesn't look like your type."

I replied, "It's really weird, but I was thinking the same thing. I can't imagine ever being attracted to him, and I have no idea what I ever saw in him."

The saying must be true, "Time heals all wounds," or maybe better said in this case, "Love is blind." So much of my memory of him must have been healed that I couldn't even determine whether she looked like him. I can't remember why or when in our relationship that I fell for him.

In June 1995, I went to the annual singles retreat at the Stonecroft Conference Center near Branson with my Sunday school class. I was asked to take my video of my first meeting with Lori and to share my story. Our minister with the singles made an announcement that anyone who wanted to see my video could come back after refreshments and watch it. I told our speaker Karl and his wife Kayla about my video so they could decide whether they wanted to see it.

They asked, "Did you know we are adoptive parents?"

I replied, "No, I didn't. My video may be too painful for you to watch; if so, I'll understand."

They said, "Thanks for inviting us. We'll watch it."

Kayla decided after a few minutes that she couldn't watch it and left the room. Not knowing what to do, I looked at Karl and said, "I'm sorry. What should I do?"

"Sharon, continue on," he said. "It is difficult for us, but we've always known of the possibility that our daughter might someday want to meet her birth mom. Meeting you just brought that realization home, even though it is difficult."

Late in July, I called Lori to let her know that I was going to be at Betty's in August with my brother Ron and his wife.

Lori had some exciting news for me: "I showed Mom the pictures of you with your sisters and Grandma when you were last here. She said, 'I'd like to meet her the next time she comes to Kansas City.' So maybe I can arrange for the two of you to meet next month."

"Yes." I was thrilled.

The date in August finally arrived when I was to meet Marge. By that time, I was a little anxious. We all met with Lori, David, Marge, and Jeanna at a restaurant. Marge had requested a public place to hopefully prevent our meeting becoming too emotional, and that was okay with me. My brother John met us. When he was introduced to Lori, he said, "I would have known you anywhere because you look so much like Sharon, although you're more beautiful in person than in the pictures."

During breakfast, Lori said something but was asked to repeat it. Marge spoke up and said, "Lori was hard to understand when she was a child."

Lori then explained, "I went to speech therapy school to learn how to pronounce my 'Rs,' and I had trouble with my brother's name. He would get mad at me when I would try to say his name. He would say, 'Just call me Boy. I'd rather you say Boy than the way you say it.'"

I was almost speechless since I had the same problem with my "Rs" when I was young. I then explained, "In school, I was always shy, and I got teased a lot because of the way I talked. I couldn't pronounce Ron's name, and I would start crying when the kids would make fun of me for saying, 'Wonnie.' I then attended speech therapy classes in the third grade where I, too, began to pronounce my 'Rs' correctly. If I would have just called him, 'Boy,' I would have saved myself some teasing."

With that exciting weekend over, I now had to hit the books again because another college semester was starting. I was anxious to get my education over with because concentrating on my classes was getting more difficult with Lori in my life. How could I make my classes more interesting and still think about her?

7

God's plan in action

O LORD, you are my God; I will exalt you and praise
your name, for in perfect faithfulness you have done
marvelous things, things planned long ago.
(Isaiah 25:1, NIV)

W hen given our term paper assignment in my Intro
to Social Work class that next semester, I thought,
*Wow! I'm going to enjoy this assignment. It'll be the
best one yet.* We were to interview a social worker. Lori was enthu-
siastic after I asked to interview her. Kathy and I drove to Kansas
City to see Lori at her workplace. When we arrived and asked to
see Lori, the receptionist asked, "Are you her mom?"

"Yes."

"I've heard so much about you. I'm glad to meet you." She
paged Lori who came to the lobby along with Jeanna and Marcia.
We discussed the events that had occurred since the day Marcia
had made that phone call to me in February.

Marcia asked, "Other than the obvious physical ones, do you and Lori share a lot of similarities in your lives?"

"Yes." A feeling of pride comes over me when someone notices the similarities in our appearance.

"Did you bring your pictures?"

"Of course," I answered. "I never know when I might run into someone who hasn't seen them."

Lori seemed amused and thrilled that I carried my miniature photo album in my purse.

Marcia went to the counter to speak to the waitress who then came back to our table. Looking at Lori and me, she said, "I can tell that you're mother and daughter. I also experienced the same thing in my life this year. I was reunited with my daughter whom I gave up for adoption nineteen years ago. We should all go on Oprah's show since we have such a beautiful story to tell."

"Lori and I discussed that possibility back in February. At that time, we both agreed it was too personal to share with everyone on television."

Lori replied, "I don't think that I would be opposed to it now, but I would only go on Oprah's show. Oprah has class and does her show tastefully."

Back at the school, Lori showed Kathy and me around the campus. I could see how wonderful Lori was with her students and how lucky the children were who attended that school. Yes, I am a little biased. She had a special touch for getting through to them. They could talk about anything with her: personal, school, social, or intimate problems.

Lori said, "One student was depressed. I gave him a tape of one of my favorite songs. I was a little frustrated over his depression since I felt I wasn't able to reach him. One day, I heard someone walking and singing down the hallway. Upon opening my door, I saw this same student singing one of the songs from the tape I had given him. The song had a positive message of being all that you can be. I just said, 'Yes!'"

On the Sunday after Thanksgiving, Lori called, "I have some news that probably won't surprise you."

"You're engaged."

"Yes. Our first date was a year ago at the Plaza to see the lights. We returned this year, and he proposed the moment the lights came on. He's such a romantic. We set our wedding for July."

For Christmas that year, I gave Lori a wooden Hallmark Christmas ornament in the shape of a toy chest. One of the toys in the chest was a train that had the year 1995 on it along with the words "Our Family" on the front. In the middle of the chest was a cutout for a picture to be inserted. I placed inside of it the picture of Lori, her mom, my mom, and me. I also got myself the same ornament.

Lori called in January to say, "I've ordered my wedding dress. David and I have started taking ballroom dance lessons on Monday nights."

"I took ballroom dance lessons in college while I was still taking fun classes before getting serious about a degree," I told her.

A week after my birthday in March, Lori sent me a postcard from Colorado. She and Jeanna spent spring break learning to ski with some friends. Knowing she took the time to send me a postcard while she was away with her friends meant a lot.

In April 1996, I completed a term paper about Lori called Sociobiology: Nature versus Nurture. While researching the material, I found a copy of a poem published in a newspaper column in 1993 that I had put away for safekeeping. I sent a copy of it to Lori, and she thought it looked familiar. She found that she had also seen that same column and placed it in her scrapbook. The poem set out the importance of both an adoptive mom and a birth mom in the life of an adopted child. Almost all of my term papers after meeting Lori involved her in some way. My conclusion to that nature versus nurture debate question was:

> Some of my genes are obvious after being around Lori. I know she wouldn't be the wonderful person she is today had it not been for her parents and their love and influence in her life.

I enjoyed this presentation more than any of the others that I did while in school. I had a big smile on my face the whole time I was speaking. Kathy was there. She had always been one of my strongest supporters. I didn't look at her because I knew she would have had tears in her eyes, and I knew I couldn't speak if I saw her tears.

In May, I went to Betty's with my mom and Evelyn for the weekend to celebrate Betty's birthday. Mom and I gave Lori our wedding gift to her: a quilt made by Mom. Royal blue was going to be her wedding color so I had purchased sixteen different pieces of printed royal blue material. Mom then cut out and appliquéd sixteen different versions of the Colonial Girl. My sisters gave her a quilt stand. Mom and I later received a card from Lori:

> Thank you both so much for my beautiful quilt. I truly appreciate the time and thoughtfulness that went into the selection of materials, the pattern, and the whole process of putting it together. We're fortunate to have come together to share these happy times. Thanks again. Love, Lori

In June, I talked to Kayla, the adoptive mother whom I had met at our singles retreat the previous year. She said, "My daughter has become interested in finding her birth mom. Thank you for sharing your story with my husband and me last year. We wouldn't have been prepared for the time our daughter finds her birth mom if you hadn't told us of your reunion story when you did."

I responded, "My thirtieth year high school reunion is tomorrow night, and I've been asked by some classmates to share my story. Please pray for me because I get so nervous when I'm asked to speak to a group."

She said, "You just continue telling your story whenever you get a chance. You'll never know how many lives are touched each time you tell it. I'll be praying for you."

The reunion was held in the school cafeteria. After our meal was over, our class president asked if anyone had anything to say. My friend and classmate Cindy thanked a few for their financial support. Looking at me, she then said, "Sharon Fieker would like to share something with the class."

If she hadn't made that statement, I probably would have chickened out. She and Judy, another classmate, both commented how they thought everyone would enjoy hearing my story because they had enjoyed hearing it.

After silently saying a prayer for strength to go along with prayers from my Sunday school class and others, I walked to the podium:

"Because I was so shy, I was prophesied in our senior year to become Mrs. America, winning the title through my speaking ability (or lack thereof). You remember those class prophecies— you know those things that could never become realities? Well, guess what? It's becoming a reality. I'm paying you back now for that prophecy."

Laughter was heard all over the room. I continued:

"Recently, my Sunday school teacher asked if we could remember the blackest time in our lives that, with God's blessing, changed to the brightest time. We all could remember such a time.

My blackest time was placing my baby daughter for adoption at her birth in 1969 without ever seeing her. My brightest time was when she found me in February 1995."

I briefly shared details about her and the news of her wedding the next month. When I sat down, a classmate whispered, "You've got guts!" I thought, *Yes, telling this beautiful story does take "guts" but God gives me the strength and wisdom to do it.*

Our class president said, "Thanks, Sharon, for sharing your story. Does anyone else wish to say anything to the class?"

A classmate who was a minister went to the podium. "I'm going to tell you about a classmate of ours who was killed in Vietnam. I received a letter from him written shortly before his death. He said he had asked his men, 'If you died today, do you know if you're going to heaven?' Think about him and ask yourselves that same question." He then sat down.

Afterward, the classmate/minister congratulated me on my reunion with Lori saying, "Thank you for having the courage to speak. I hadn't planned on saying anything, but I felt the nudge to do so after you spoke."

Remembering how many people were praying for me that evening, I thought, God surely does answer prayers. Although I'm not a professional speaker, I just have to be willing.

Judy said, "Sharon, I was watching our classmates while you were speaking. You had the complete attention of everyone. They seemed supportive and interested. I'm so proud of you."

The next day, I couldn't wait to tell Lori about my high school reunion. I asked how her wedding plans were coming along. Thinking about her wedding made me wonder, *Will I be able to handle the emotions that will go along with it?* It doesn't matter. I can't wait.

the wedding

For this reason a man will leave his father and mother and
be united to his wife, and the two will become one flesh.
(Ephesians 5:31, NIV)

*L*ori's wedding came. My mom, my sisters, one brother,
their spouses, and I arrived at the church. Lori's mom
Marge was loving and supportive. She could have had
an attitude, "Tonight is my night, not yours. I'm Lori's mother."
Instead, she came to me as soon as I got inside the church, hugged
me, and told me how beautiful I looked. Lori's brother Chris joined
us, and Marge introduced us.

That night, I was on an emotional roller-coaster ride that
was the most difficult I had experienced since our reunion, but I
wouldn't have missed it. I wasn't part of the wedding party, just a
guest. Being a guest was more than I had ever dreamed possible
prior to our reunion. Just think, I went twenty-five years without

knowing anything about my daughter to sitting in a church watching the most beautiful bride I had ever seen walk down the aisle.

The minister asked, "Who giveth away the bride?"

Lori's brother answered, "Her mother and I."

Hearing that response, I thought, *Marge and I have always had one thing in common—our #1 concern being Lori's happiness. This time was no different. Marge was giving away her daughter so she could be happy with her husband just as I had given Lori away at her birth so she could be happy with both a loving mother and father.*

I enjoyed the receiving line more than at any other wedding. Lori and David stood in front of the cake and punch table greeting their guests. Noticing Lori's tears when it was my turn in line, I gave her a hug and congratulated her.

My stomach was in knots from about an hour before and an hour after the wedding. Emotions I wasn't proud of bounced back and forth so my stomach felt like a punching bag. I was thrilled and honored being there watching my beautiful daughter on the happiest day of her life. Just as quickly, I thought of all the times I had missed in her life and asked myself how I could have given her up. Then, I would recover and think how happy she was and that I had allowed her a beautiful life by making an adoption plan for her. Watching Lori that night, I knew I could take some credit for her beautiful smile.

The hardest part came when they played a song at the reception for the "mother of the bride." Marge led that next dance. Keeping in mind this song was not meant to hurt me, I reminded myself that it was a way to honor Marge. Lori's dad died two years prior to our reunion, so I can only imagine how difficult the night was for Marge in many ways.

At the reception, Marge said, "Sharon, I want you to meet

my sister and brother-in-law, and also my neighbors whom we've known since Lori was three."

Marge's neighbor said, "When we first met, Lori was outgoing and so cute with her curly hair." Hearing about Lori's life at that age was enjoyable.

With a big hug, Marge's sister said, "Sharon, I'm so happy to meet you. Thank you for being here. If it weren't for you, we wouldn't be here tonight."

The emotions that night that I wasn't so proud of were those of being left out of the wedding. Anyone else in the same circumstances, if they were honest, would have felt them also. When my more realistic emotions kicked in, I knew everything was handled appropriately. That was Lori's big night. Few people there knew me except for Lori's family and her closest friends. Imagine what would have happened had an announcement been made or the rumors spread that I was Lori's birth mom. I wouldn't have wanted that kind of attention on the most important day of her life.

The first year of our reunion was the toughest with such roller-coaster emotions. At first, I would worry every time I didn't hear from her. Would I hear from her again? I would also worry about what I would or should say to her. Maybe her curiosity had been filled now, and she might not want me any longer. She and I both went through a lot of changes that first year. We both could have sent the stress monitors completely off the charts. Time has a way of healing emotions, and I spent time in prayer. Life was great when the up-and-down emotions of the roller-coaster ride got stuck in the up mode. Fortunately for Lori and me, these up emotions have become more prevalent for us as the years have passed.

If you are a birth mom contemplating going to your child's wedding, I would suggest you think back to the time you placed your child for adoption. Did you want your child to have a better life than what you could provide? My feelings about attending Lori's wedding were that this day could possibly be the most important day of her life. I wanted to be there for her, regardless of how difficult it might have seemed to me. Yes, I was uncomfortable and the event was difficult, but the rewards of seeing her as a bride made my pain seem bearable.

A birth mom from one of my online mailing lists posted that very question since she was going to attend her daughter's wedding. She asked if any other birth mom had considered not going to her child's wedding because of the pain being too great.

My response was, "You should go. You will get only one chance to be at your daughter's wedding." After replying, I also forwarded a copy of my message to Lori so she could read my description of the wedding and how emotional it was for me. She later told me, "I cried when I read your message about my wedding, but I'm glad that you sent it to me. You did a beautiful job in explaining it."

Getting her approval on my writing is always an added plus.

My niece Kayleen lived about thirty minutes away from Lori's house, and she invited Lori and David to her house while I was there for Christmas. Lori gave me a picture frame that had a beautiful angel and child bordering its side. The angel reminded me of God having His protective angels around her as an answer to my prayer the day I placed her for adoption.

Lori's wedding was my big event for that year. Now that the year had ended, what would the New Year bring? My life seemed to focus on one big event after another. Possibly, the next big event would be the completion of my education and then graduation.

sharing my testimony

> I will write down all these things as a testimony of what
> the LORD will do. I will entrust it to my disciples, who
> will pass it down to future generations.
> (Isaiah 8:16, NLT)

Kathy and I were in our last semester of college and were allowed to work jointly on our senior research project. We named it Birth Mothers: Relinquishment and Relationships. We sent out and received questionnaires back from four birth moms locally along with thirty-eight birth moms from two online mailing lists. The local birth moms had been referred to me by their family members or friends who had heard my reunion story.

During our oral presentation to the class, I was asked, "Was working on such a personal project difficult?"

I responded, "Having worked so closely with other women who knew and understood my feelings was rewarding and healing."

One birth mom thanked us for letting her answer the questionnaire and added, "No one else had ever cared enough to ask even when I was willing to discuss it."

Kathy said, "Once you get on the mailing lists, you will be hooked and will want to stay on them long after our class ends." She was right. A newly reunited birth mom would write and ask questions from those of us who had already experienced a reunion. We would tell of our feelings at the time. An online support group was formed about that same time that was started by two birth moms, and I joined it. They had felt the need to start a group made up of Christian members of the adoption triad.

Mother's Day that year was a busy and exciting day. During graduation ceremonies, I received a Bachelor of Science degree in criminal justice, psychology, and sociology. An article was published in the paper that day:

From a shell, heart emerges

With the immense amount of help and support given unwed mothers today, it must seem incredible to young people that folk singer Joni Mitchell just recently acknowledged a daughter she bore out of wedlock 32 years ago. "The main thing at the time was to conceal it," she said. "You have no idea what the stigma was." Mitchell's revelation wasn't so surprising to those of us who grew up during the 1960s. We were on the cusp of the Age of Aquarius, with rock 'n' roll exhorting the passion and intensity of young love at every throb of the car radio, yet, when young women became pregnant, those who didn't marry often left home, had their babies, and kept their secrets. We were at the mercy of conflicting cultural value systems, value systems readying themselves for the war they found during the late 1960s and early 1970s. People like Sharon Fieker and her daughter Lori Smith were the casualties.

Sharon was a senior in high school when I was a freshman, a

good student, a "salt of the earth" kind of kid, one of 11 children. I hadn't seen her since then, when she called last week to tell me that two years ago the daughter she had given up at birth in 1969 had found her, and she was ecstatic. She has worked at the Springfield Police Department for 22 years, and is now a records supervisor.

For 25 years Sharon told no one about Lori's birth except close family members. For 25 years, Sharon collected turtles, so many she thinks about adding another room to her home just to hold them. Looking back, she believes they were tangible symbols of the shell under which she buried her secret. "I didn't talk about this all those years," she says. "I'd allow myself to think about it only when I was by myself—I'd see a movie about adoption with a friend, and I wouldn't say anything, then I'd cry myself to sleep."

Two years ago Lori's adoptive mother gave Lori her adoption papers. They included Sharon's last name and that she was from Springfield, and Lori easily located Sharon. A co-worker of Lori's called Sharon to see if she was receptive to meeting Lori, and Lori drove to Springfield. The two became fast friends immediately, and Sharon is amazed at the practical, caring young woman her daughter—a social worker in Kansas City—became.

Sharon shakes her head and laughs when she remembers Lori's concern for her the first time they met. Sitting in Sharon's living room, Lori asked about her father, the man Sharon had dated for six months and who disappeared after she told him she was pregnant. "She leaned over and put her hand on my knee and said, 'Now, if this is too painful, we don't have to discuss it.' Within an hour, she started telling me about her own relationships. It was as if she told me that to tell me it was all right, she understood."

The intense happiness she has felt since finding Lori has taught Sharon how profoundly having to keep her secret affected her. She had always been shy, the one to whom everyone else told their problems, yet she never shared her own. She had some long-term relationships, but never married. "I would ask everything about them, but wouldn't tell them anything about me. If you don't trust other people enough to share personal things, you don't have much of a relationship."

Now, she says, she talks endlessly about her own life, a life that is complete, a life in which she sees her past and her future mirrored in her daughter. "I smile at everyone I see." It's in their smiles, people tell her, where Lori and Sharon look most alike.

Such a happy outcome. But at such a price.

Today Sharon will stand at church, as she has for the previous two Mother's Days since Lori found her, when the pastor asks mothers to be recognized. I'll be thinking of her, and saying my own thanks that the shame of a society's sexual double standard is no longer broken on the backs of young, kind girls who fall in love.

Sarah Overstreet is associate editorial page editor of the News-Leader.[3]

Although I had reviewed the article before it was submitted by Sarah, I wasn't prepared for the tears as I read it. The day ended on a perfect note with a phone call from Lori. Wishing me a happy Mother's Day, she asked about graduation and the newspaper article. Her closing statement was, "I'm so proud of you! Keep smiling that beautiful smile that everyone is always telling you about."

A week later, a lady from my church wrote a letter to the editor concerning Sarah's article:

OVERSTREET: Subject of column definition of strength

Occasionally I find an article in the News-Leader that makes me think I got my money's worth. Such was the case Mother's Day, May 11, after reading Sarah Overstreet's "From a shell, heart emerges."

Sarah's writing has long been a favorite of mine. Knowing Sharon Fieker and even knowing Sarah would be featuring Sharon in her column still didn't prepare me for the beautiful and moving account of Sharon's long-kept secret and eventual glad reunion with her daughter, Lori.

In today's "tell-all" world, Sharon's story has a special significance. It takes a rare strength of character and integrity to make a difficult decision and live with the consequences solitarily. It takes grace, sensitivity, and maturity to take a heart-held secret from the protection of a shell into the light of day.

Sharon has moved courageously through grief, sadness, and disappointment. She also possesses modesty and humility, which may be why no mention was made that, also on Mother's Day, Sharon graduated cum laude from Drury College.

Instead of letting "what might have been" be her life's theme, Sharon decided to invest herself in her family and friends and in her career and church. Now, happily, she can share all she has become with her child.

Linda Agee, Springfield[4]

Not knowing the letter was going to be written, I was touched by the time and thought that went into it.

A month later, I told Kathy, "I think I'm in the wrong career. I need to listen to people's problems and get paid for it. While shopping, a shoe salesman told me his life story—anyway, the divorce segment of it. He spoke of the court battle, the settlement, and the ugly mess."

Kathy responded, "Well, Sharon, you have that special smile that causes people to confide in you. Remember the classmates in those presentations ignored the others in the classroom, even the professor, and just seemed to be talking personally to you?"

Until she mentioned it, I wasn't aware that anyone else had noticed that the students seemed to be speaking to me personally. It had seemed as though no one else was in the room but me. I have to say that of all of my traits that Lori could have inherited, I believe she received my best one: my smile.

The first local support group meeting of six birth moms met in June 1997. We shared our stories and decided to meet again the next month. While in Kansas City in September, I met two birth moms for breakfast. Then, I met Lori for lunch at another mall. We talked a lot about adoption-related issues that we had never been able to discuss before. In the two years since we had met, she and I had little time alone. We had seen each other about every two to three months, but we were always with her family or mine. That day was filled with quality time for us.

Lori told me, "The one thing that I feared the most in contacting you that first time was that you would try to take over as my mom. I knew we'd have a problem if you did because I love my mom so much. We didn't discuss it the first day we met, but it was clear to me within a few minutes and without your realizing it. Because you had so much love and respect for my mom, I knew there wouldn't be a problem. Although Mom hasn't told you in so many words, I know she has nothing but love and respect for you. You allowed her a chance to have a child, a child that she wouldn't have had otherwise."

Lori and I discussed her birth father Bob. She said, "He's not a big concern with me. I know how hard you've tried to find him."

I assured her, "Although he's difficult to find, I'll keep trying so you can have your medical history."

While walking around the mall with Lori, I told her, "Lori, I've had a wonderful day, first with meeting two birth moms, then with my favorite daughter, and ending with meeting four other birth moms in Overland Park."

"Yeah, right, I'm your only daughter!" Lori said.

In February 1998, Lori planned to stay overnight at my house so she could attend a work-related conference. This trip was her first to my house since the day we had met in February 1995. I asked her if she would object to an open-house celebration at my house so that she and my friends could meet.

Thirty-three people came to my open house—church friends, coworkers, family, and close friends. Three of my friends from high school—Gloria, Cindy, and Judy—took care of nearly everything so I could greet my guests. Lori loved meeting them. My guests included three of my new birth mom friends. I overheard Lori telling one of them how proud she was of me for what I was doing to help birth moms.

After the guests left, Lori asked about meeting my coworkers, so we went to my workplace. Over lunch the next day, Lori met four long-time friends who weren't able to attend the night before. Later, she said, "You have some wonderful friends."

"Yes, I do. I feel lucky to have them."

She said, "Well, it is obvious they have a good friend in you, too. You have to be a good friend to have a good friend."

After Lori returned home, she sent me a card, saying:

> Sharon, Thanks again for letting me stay with you and for the open house. I enjoyed meeting your friends. The number of friends you have is a tribute to the kind of person you are: a great friend. Have a good week. Love, Lori

10

speaking ministry continues

If anyone speaks, he should do it as one speaking the very
words of God. If anyone serves, he should do it with the
strength God provides, so that in all things God may be
praised through Jesus Christ. To him be the glory and the
power for ever and ever. Amen.
(1 Peter 4:11, NIV)

*E*very Mother's Day has been special since 1995. How
could another one ever compare to those I've already
experienced? To celebrate Mother's Day 1998, I spoke
at Ron's church for a mother-daughter luncheon. I told of the
harmonious reunion between Lori and me. Ron's wife said, "I
got teary-eyed, but I tried not to let you see me. I was afraid you
wouldn't be able to speak."

My mom went with me. She had called earlier in the week
to say, "I'd love to go with you. If you think it would be more

difficult for you to talk with me there, however, I'll understand and won't go."

At the end of my testimony, one lady asked, "What about your feelings and reactions the week between the call and the time you first saw Lori?"

I replied, "I was a basket case. I couldn't do anything but cry."

Mom asked if she could add something. "I want everyone to know how proud I am of Sharon and how thrilled I am to get to know Lori. After all of these years, I'm also happy that Sharon is back in church."

Now, it was time for more tears.

Ron asked me if I would consider speaking again at a missions meeting where men and women from different churches, not just his church, would attend. Since his wife had just heard me speak, I asked her, "Do you think I should speak again? Would it be appropriate for a missions meeting?"

"It would be wonderful. Don't change a thing," she said.

Several weeks later, I spoke at the missions meeting. I had wondered how Ron was going to tie my story in with missions. He introduced me: "We usually think of a foreign mission when we first hear the word mission, but a mission begins at home. The Jesus in us is sometimes the only Jesus some people ever see throughout their daily lives. I'm proud of my sister Sharon for the way she has handled her life and because she is willing to tell her story, one that I'm sure will bless everyone here."

Fearing I wouldn't be able to speak because he kept going on about how proud he was of me, I wanted to give him the time-out signal. As I spoke, I noticed tears throughout from the men as well as the women.

"To keep me on track, I'll use note cards; otherwise, we might be here all night," I told the audience.

Ron said after I finished, "I have to comment about Sharon's rambling on and on. She used to be shy and rarely talked. Now, our family rarely gets a word in when she's around. There's one thing that bothers me though: I'm worried about how our family will ever be able to cope when the time comes for her to show pictures and brag about a grandchild."

After learning that I had spoken at Ron's church, Norma asked, "Would you speak at my church in Kansas City?"

Norma talked to her pastor and briefly told him about my story. Not knowing whether my story would fit in with his Sunday morning services, he asked, "What kind of church does she attend? What about her emotional state throughout all of this?"

Noticing his reluctance, she gave him a copy of my testimony. "Read this and then get back with me. She'll be here next weekend," Norma said.

Her pastor called her the next morning, "We definitely want your aunt to speak."

Norma called me, "Both the pastor and the assistant pastor want you to speak next Sunday."

To confirm the date, the pastor called, "I was touched by your testimony. You have a gift for words. You express yourself in a wonderful way. I'm excited about your agreeing to speak."

Knowing Lori was going to be there to hear me, I thought I would be more nervous. I saw her wiping her tears. If possible, I believe I smiled even more with her there. Just before expressing my appreciation to the congregation for being so attentive, I asked, "Now may I introduce my daughter Lori?"

She had agreed to stand as long as she didn't have to say anything. She stood up and turned around. It was an awesome moment.

I had e-mailed my online birth mom friends in the Kansas City area that I would be speaking, and one of them attended. She said,

"I cried from the minute you stood up until you finished. The lady in front of me must have been a birth mom, too, because she cried from the moment you mentioned adoption until you finished."

Although the church's program was entitled, "The Shell Within," no one knew about the subject of my story. The couple singing the special song during both services told me they got teary-eyed during the second service and could hardly sing. They sang before I spoke during the first service so they weren't aware of the content of my story. The second time, however, they realized how much their words matched my story. I felt the LORD leading the services that morning. Their song described how you have to give love away in order to keep it.

I asked Lori at lunch the next day what she thought of the services.

She replied, "You did a wonderful job. If you were nervous, you didn't let it show. You arranged everything into a beautiful story. I almost asked my mom to attend, but I was afraid it would bother you so I didn't. When you speak again in the Kansas City area, I want to hear you, and I want my mom to hear you."

Over lunch, Lori and I again discussed her birth father. I told her, "Trying to find him is like looking for a needle in a haystack. His name is just too common. There are over two hundred guys with the same name in every state. Every road I take to try to find him seems like the wrong one."

Lori said, "I don't want to interfere in his life. I'm not sure I even want a relationship with him. I would like to see him and obtain his medical history; anything beyond that, I don't know. It'll be okay if you can't find him. I appreciate all of the work you've done so far."

Knowing she was being nice for my sake but that she needed his medical history, I knew I would keep trying to find him.

11

finding Lori's birth father

And we know that in all things God works for the
good of those who love him, who have been
called according to his purpose.
(Romans 8:28, NIV)

*I*n July 1998, my brother Jerry and his wife asked me to meet them at Zio's Restaurant so that I could meet their friend Roger. Although Roger and I had not been enthused about their attempts at matchmaking, we agreed to meet. I couldn't believe it when I learned he had written a story that had been published, and he enjoyed writing. We were still talking several hours later although Jerry and Darla had left after an hour. I knew he was special the minute I told him about Lori and noticed the tears in his eyes. That was a switch for me to tell a guy about Lori so soon after meeting him. I felt that he could become an important person to me and a good friend. He helped me to see a male perspective and offered good advice in talking to Lori's birth father if

I found him, considering that thirty years had passed. I feel certain that meeting a Christian man with whom I could enjoy a friendship outside of a sexual relationship caused God to smile.

Remembering the conversation I had with Pam, my friend from St. Louis who had also known Bob, I decided to once again try to find him. Pam had told me that Beth and Benjamin, Bob's great-aunt and uncle, had lost a son. He had been killed in a freak accident in their hometown. My friend Kathy from high school and I had spent a weekend there during the time that Bob and I were dating. Bob had met us there because it was also his hometown. Knowing about the online Social Security Death Index for obtaining death records, I had tried the previous year to find out some information about the accident. At that time, however, I couldn't find anything. Trying in July 1998, I found the information. The social security number had been issued in the State of Missouri, so I felt sure this was the same person I had known. I called the library in that city to obtain a copy of the accident report. The friendly librarian said she would mail the information to me.

Several weeks later, I received the newspaper clipping describing the accident and also the obituary page. The librarian attached a note, "After reading the obituary, I recognized the name and the accident. I checked and obtained Beth and Benjamin's address for you." Since a telephone number wasn't listed in her note, I made some calls and found their number along with some added information. Thank God for librarians and others who are friendly and helpful.

On one of the calls I made, I said, "When I knew Beth and Benjamin in St. Louis, I also knew their nephew Bob. Do you know him?"

She replied, "Well, honey, do you mean Billy Bob?"

I couldn't believe it. Having spent three years trying to find him, thinking Bob was his first name, I now had his address and phone number. My heart was racing. This information was falling into place so quickly and easily. As soon as I had his correct name, I double-checked the online database I had been checking for three years. He was listed.

The next morning, I called Beth. She seemed thrilled to hear from me and asked, "Do you know what day this is? It was twenty-two years ago today since our son died. What a nightmare. I had dreaded to get up this morning knowing what would be ahead if it should be anything like the past twenty-two years. Your call lifted my spirits, and it's truly a godsend."

If you only knew, I thought. I now understood why I couldn't find the information the year before; I had to wait for God's timing.

I told Beth about Lori. She was shocked, "I'm so sorry you had to bear the burden of being pregnant alone. I didn't know anything about it. I wish you would have told me when you stayed with us. Bob and Benjamin had always been close. In fact, Bob had moved to St. Louis because of Benjamin. We haven't, however, spoken to him since the early '80s."

I told her Lori has beautiful hair just like her youngest daughter did when she was little.

She asked, "Does Lori look like Bob or you?"

"She probably looks a little like him, but you'll have to tell me your opinion after you see her pictures. When Lori asked me about him, I told her I couldn't see any distinct features that she had that reminded me of him. Beth, it's just been too many years since I've seen him to know. I'll give you my web site address so you can view the pictures and get back with me."

She asked, "Is Lori as tall as Bob?"

"She's 5'8", the same as me."

"Bob married a girl named Brenda, and they have a son named

Brent. I'll help you in any way possible, except making contact with Bob. Benjamin and I haven't been home for some time, so I really don't know a lot about him. It's been too many years."

Not wanting Bob to hear about Lori from anyone except me, I dialed his number. I prayed for wisdom. My pulse rate would have probably sent the monitors off the charts. After all, I hadn't talked to him for almost thirty years. Brenda answered, "Hello."

"Is Bob there?"

"He's sleeping since he works the night shift. What do you want with him anyway?"

"I'm Sharon Fieker," I said. "I also work nights, so I understand the inconvenience of my call. I am sorry for disturbing him. Beth and Benjamin were friends of mine in St. Louis, and I also knew Bob. I talked to Beth earlier today. Now, I need to talk to Bob."

She said, "We haven't talked to them for years. I hope they're okay. I can hear Bob getting up. It'll just be a minute."

Hearing Bob in the background coming into the room, I could also hear Brenda say something about Beth and Benjamin. What should I say? Would he remember our last night together?

Bob then groggily answered the phone.

"This is Sharon Fieker. Do you remember me?"

"Yes."

"I'm sorry for waking you. I also work nights, so I understand how difficult it is to try to carry on a conversation after having just awakened. So I'll just get to the point. Do you remember the last time I saw you when I told you I was pregnant?"

"Yes." Bob answered with a questioning tone as though he might be afraid of what could be next.

I thought, *I'm glad he remembers me.* I then followed with, "I didn't know what to do. I wanted my baby to have both a loving mother and a father and a better life than what I could provide, so I placed her for adoption." I thought, *That's a long sentence, but I got it out.*

Continuing on, "She found me in 1995, and she told me she had a lot of love and respect for my decision. Because of me, she had a wonderful life with loving parents. She's absolutely beautiful. I realize I'm a little biased. She has hair as curly as your niece did when she was little."

Realizing I was rambling and that Bob hadn't said much, I said, "You're probably in an awkward position with your wife standing close by wondering what's going on?"

He answered, "Yes."

I continued, "Lori would like to see you. She wants to see what you look like and to get your medical history since I couldn't help her with that information. She doesn't want to interfere in your life. She got married two years ago, and I feel she deserves this information."

Again, he answered, "Yes."

"I heard you were married and that you have one son?"

"Yes."

"Do you have a computer with Internet access?"

"Yes." I was glad he occasionally said something, so that I knew he hadn't passed out from the shock.

"I have a web site with our reunion story on it. You can check it out to see if you notice any striking resemblance. I can give you the address."

"I can't take it down right now."

"Do you want my phone number so you can call after you've had time to process this?"

"Yes." After giving him my phone number, I hung up the phone and breathed a sign of relief. My searching for three years was over. Bob had been found.

Not being able to wait another minute, I called Lori:

"Hello. This is Sharon. Are you sitting down?"

"No, should I be?"

"Yes."

"Okay. I'm sitting down."

"I've found Bob."

She exclaimed, "Oh, gosh! Oh, my gosh! How did that happen? Did you talk to him?"

Telling her everything about the phone calls, she replied, "Wow! I don't know how I feel about him. Thanks for all of the work you've done in finding him."

I told her, "He said he has one son whose name is Brent."

Lori replied, "Oh, I hadn't even thought of that possibility. I have a brother."

I continued, "Before I talked to Bob, I contacted Beth. It felt wonderful to be able to help her get through the day on the anniversary of her son's death. You understand how it feels since you help so many in your job."

"Yes, I think we're a lot alike. Your timing couldn't have been more perfect. David and I have recently started talking about wanting to have children."

Lori had told me once that she and David wanted children eventually, but they didn't know when eventually would be, possibly five years. She added, "Having my complete medical history from both sides will be wonderful to have when I have my next doctor's appointment. Thanks again for talking to him and finding out about his history."

Bob didn't call again to obtain further information about Lori. Beth called me after several weeks, "Have you heard from Bob yet? Benjamin doesn't believe he'll ever call since he wasn't curious for almost thirty years about whether you had kept your child, had an abortion, or just what had happened. After I told Benjamin about your call, he was so angry with Bob. I believe he could have killed him if he would have been here. You must hate him for abandoning you."

I confessed, "I did for many years, but I've had a change of heart the last few years. How could I hate someone who had given me something as precious as a child? Carrying all of that hate was making me an angry person. I had to get rid of it. I'm like a new person. God gave me strength and wisdom to forgive."

Knowing it would take some time for Bob to sort out just what he would do, or what his wife said he should do, we waited. After a few weeks, however, I started thinking Benjamin might be right. For my sake, I didn't care if he ever made contact. For Lori's sake, however, I hoped that he would. I knew she needed all of the medical history she could obtain, especially now that she was trying to get pregnant.

I felt calm about locating Bob for Lori, and I was glad that I had learned about forgiveness and God's love. I had found him. Now my part was over. Right?

forgiveness

Bear with each other and forgive whatever
grievances you may have against one another.
Forgive as the Lord forgave you.
(Colossians 3:13, NIV)

*I*n September, Lori asked, "Have you heard anything from
Bob? It would be interesting to know what his reasons are
for not wanting to see me."

I replied, "Well, I guess I could write him."

She said, "I was hoping you would say that. Although I thought
about it, you're so much better at writing letters than I am."

Knowing how important it was to Lori, I mailed Bob a letter by
restricted delivery to ensure he received it:

> Bob, Since I haven't heard anything further from you since
> my telephone call on August 4, I thought I would send some
> information to you about Lori. In case you're still contem-

plating contacting her, I wanted to give you her address so you don't have to call me to get it.

Again, Bob, I want to reiterate that Lori doesn't want to cause any problems for you. She's aware that receiving news about her might have caused you some problems or unexpected stress; however, that wasn't her intent. She's interested in your medical history.

Lori and her husband are ready to start a family, and she'd like to have this information. She was thrilled to know that I had finally contacted you after searching for three years. She was excited at the chance that she could go to her doctor with actual family history information. All of her life she's had to tell her doctor, "I don't know. I was adopted." I feel she has a right to this information.

As I told you, Lori is curious as to whether she looks like you. I'm not much help because I don't have any pictures of you. My sister does have an old home movie that was made at Perry's birthday party. (Remember those old projectors instead of videos?) Although Lori has looked at it, she was unable to see your facial features close enough to know if she looks like you. Lori has been told she looks like me; but, of course, I feel she must have some of your features.

So that you can see for yourself how beautiful Lori is, I'm sending some pictures of her. She is as beautiful on the inside and such a delight to be with. She is a happily well-adjusted young lady. She is a school social worker in Kansas City, a position that is well suited for her. She has such love and compassion for those kids that is typical of her wonderful personality. Yes, I am biased where she is concerned. She is the best thing that has ever happened to me, and I love her very much. She has brought so much joy into my life.

My web site is listed above in my return address. Since you said you have a computer with Internet access, you may wish to view some pictures of Lori.

As you can imagine from this long letter, I like to write. I graduated from college last year after years of working and going to evening college. After Lori found me, nearly every term paper I completed was about her in some way. I'm also contemplating writing a book about our wonderful reunion.

Well, Bob, I must hush for now before I get too overwhelmed with rambling on about Lori. I hope you contact her soon so that she can have this important medical history. Maybe some day you will find it in your heart to meet her face to face so that she can know something more than just a name. Thanks for giving me the most precious gift anyone could have: A daughter. Sharon

I received a telephone call a few evenings later: "Sharon?"
"Yes."
"This is Bob."
I thought, *Okay, you have my full attention.* I breathed a prayer for wisdom.

Bob continued, "I'm sorry for being so long in getting back with you, but I've been going through a lot recently. Just so you will know—my wife is on the other line." I thought, *And your point is?* I wondered whether he had told her before they had gotten married that he had fathered a child or if she had only learned about Lori the day that I called him or the day he received my letter.

I just replied, "That's okay. There's no problem here."

In sort of a suspicious tone, he asked, "Just what was your intention in having me sign for that letter?"

"Well, Bob, think about it. Since I haven't heard from you for seven weeks, I wanted to be sure you got the letter. I didn't want to always wonder if you got it."

He replied with a friendlier tone, "Oh, okay." He then adamantly stated, "I don't want my son or my mom to know anything about her for now. My son isn't old enough or mature enough to understand."

"Bob, how old is he?"

"Twenty-five."

"That's not a problem. Lori isn't out to hurt you or your family or cause you any problems. She just wants your medical history and maybe to be able to look at you. Knowing their roots is so important to adoptees."

Bob said, "I've been fortunate so far. There's not a lot of medical history, but I'll give you what there is."

I asked, "Did you look at my web site?"

"Yes, but I haven't had time to read every word of it."

"Because of our smiles, I know Lori looks a lot like me."

"Yes, that's quite obvious."

"I kind of think her eyes possibly look like yours."

"Yes, that was the first thing I noticed," Bob said.

"I really can't remember what you looked like. It's been too many years."

"That's understandable. I'm fifty-two, and my memory is getting worse," Bob replied.

We all laughed.

I said, "I turned fifty in March so I know now what it's like to be over fifty."

Brenda said, "I'm only forty-seven, and I'm always teasing him about being an old man."

Laughingly, I replied, "I understand that."

Bob then asked, "Does she feel any animosity toward me? She certainly would have that right. I wouldn't do anything to hurt her; I've done enough already."

"No, Bob, she doesn't hate you nor does she want to cause you any problems," I said. "The day we first met, she put her hand on my knee and said, 'This may be too painful for you to talk about. If so, I'll understand, but I just have to ask about my birth father.' I told her, 'There's not anything you can't ask me. No, it's not too painful. Too many years have passed.' Bob, I'm explaining this to you so you'll know how considerate she really is. She's always thinking of someone else's feelings. She's the most levelheaded and considerate person I've ever met." I then started to go on and on about her, but then I added, "Well, I've already told you that in the letter."

Bob said, "Yes, and you're probably a little biased. How tall is she?"

"She's 5'8." Do you have any recent pictures?"

"No, it's been a few years."

Brenda said, "We're not much into picture taking."

I thought, *What a shame since Lori loves pictures.*

Bob then jokingly said, "Well as far as your book is concerned, just know that I don't want to become a famous person because of it."

I then laughed and replied, "You don't have anything to worry about. I don't plan on giving enough information about you to identify you."

He asked, "Do you have a pen handy so that you can write?"

"Yes." He didn't realize I was taking notes so I wouldn't forget anything he said so I could tell Lori.

Giving me his e-mail address, he said, "You can contact me through that any time you want. But please don't send any more letters through the mail. I live near my mother, and my mailbox is at her place."

"I'll give your address to Lori along with the rest of the information you gave me. Thank you for calling. Bye."

I then called Lori and told her everything Bob said.

"I'm surprised he called so quickly after you sent the letter," Lori said.

"What did you think of my letter?"

Lori replied, "It was beautiful. You did an excellent job. It sounds like he doesn't want contact."

"No, Lori, it didn't sound like that to me. He didn't say he wasn't going to ever tell his mom or his son; he just didn't want them to know for now."

"Yes, that's true," she said.

"He wouldn't have given me his e-mail address for you if he hadn't wanted contact," I reminded her.

"Well, yes, I guess you're right. I guess I could send him a short message this weekend and thank him for the information he gave you."

I responded, "I think that's a good idea. It would be a good way of breaking the ice and getting off to a good start."

Lori mailed me a copy of the message that she e-mailed to Bob a few days after my conversation with him:

> Dear Bob, I just wanted to send you a quick note to say thank you for responding to Sharon's letter last week. She mailed me a copy of the letter that she sent to you so that I would know what she had said. I think she expressed exactly what I had hoped, and what I would have written had I done it myself. I don't know if she told you but when I first came in contact with her, I had one of my co-workers call the first time. I did this because I wanted to respect her wishes, in case she didn't want contact with me. Fortunately, she did, and we met two weeks later. I don't blame you for wanting to hold off sharing this news with your son and mother.
>
> Actually, I really didn't have the nerve or courage to search very hard until after my father passed away in September of 1992. He was very sensitive about the adoption issue, and I know he would have taken it as a personal insult, had I told

him I was curious about finding my biological parents. My mother, on the other hand, could understand my curiosity. I think it was in 1994 that I brought up the topic with her, and she gave me my adoption papers that had Sharon's last name on them. With her being one of 11 children, mostly boys and from a rural farming area, it wasn't difficult to find her family members in the phone book. Enough of that story though, maybe another time.

Anyway, I was sharing with Sharon recently how ironic and fortunate it was that she found you at this time. My husband and I have recently begun trying to start our family, and I am very thankful to have more information about both sides of my biological history. I am also thankful that there aren't any alarming genetic concerns or issues on either side thus far.

I would like to assure you both that I don't have any intention or desire to create any discomfort, stress, or embarrassment for you. I'm sure that you will tell whomever in your family whatever you think is appropriate about me whenever the time is right; if that time ever comes. That is none of my business. We laugh about it now, but honestly, when I found Sharon, something that went through both of our minds before we met was, "What if this person is basically 'trashy' and all she wants is to leech onto me for my money, and ruin my life?" (Kind of a Jerry Springer episode concept.) Fortunately, that was not the case.

Sharon and I talk on the phone, send messages on the computer, send cards, and letters. Since she has a sister here, along with nieces and nephews in Kansas City, we see each other about once a month or so. We have a nice friendship; she has also met my Mom, and they get along well. I have shared with Sharon many times, and I want you to know, too, that I could not have had better parents than the ones I have; even if you and Sharon had been given the opportunity to hand pick them yourselves. When I think about what my life might have been like had Sharon chosen to keep me, I realize

I would have had a nice life filled with a lot of love and a large caring, extended family. However, I probably would not have had many of the opportunities and experiences I've had while growing up in Kansas City with my adoptive family. I think Sharon and I agree that her decision was a good one. I do not blame you for the past. In my opinion, things were a lot different in 1969. For all we know, had you stayed with Sharon because you felt guilty or obligated, but not for love, the two of you probably would have divorced anyway. That is something that no child needs to experience! So once again, I'm glad everything turned out the way it did.

As you can tell, I received Sharon's gift of rambling on and on. She and I really do have a lot in common. Actually, I found it intriguing that you said I have your eyes. My hair, my smile, and my eyes are the main features I receive compliments on. If you ever feel comfortable with it, I would like to see a picture of all three of you. (I love pictures.) I would like to see for myself the resemblances we share. Well, I really should let you go. I'm sure this whole past week has been a little overwhelming for you and Brenda. I don't want to scare you away by writing a novel the first time. Please feel free to write back if you would like. We don't check the computer every day, but at least 2 or 3 times a week.

Please take care, and I hope to hear from you when or if you feel comfortable contacting me. Sincerely, Lori

A short time after that, I said, "Lori, I like my way the best, that of telling everyone and anyone, even strangers, about you. It's better than worrying about what anyone might think about me. If Bob could meet you and get to know you, I'm sure he would change his mind. He, too, would then want everyone to know and love you just as I do."

Now that I had found Bob and had accomplished that mission, where would the next step lead? At times, I felt like Dorothy going down the yellow brick road. My life was so exciting and scary at the same time. Because I knew that God had a plan for my life, I tried to turn those anxieties over to Him.

13

God will make a way

There is a time for everything, and a season for every activity under heaven: a time to be born and a time to die, a time to plant and a time to uproot, a time to kill and a time to heal, a time to tear down and a time to build, a time to weep and a time to laugh, a time to mourn and a time to dance, a time to scatter stones and a time to gather them, a time to embrace and a time to refrain, a time to search and a time to give up, a time to keep and a time to throw away, a time to tear and a time to mend, a time to be silent and a time to speak, a time to love and a time to hate, a time for war and a time for peace.
(Ecclesiastes 3:1–8, NIV)

*B*eing concerned about what would happen next in the reunion process shouldn't have bothered me. Things have a way of falling into place. Lori's friend Jeanna contacted me about coming to Springfield during November and staying with me, as she had some meetings to attend. I wondered if it might be awkward without Lori being present, but it wasn't. The fact that she stayed with me meant a lot to me and demonstrated to me she was comfortable enough with our friendship to stay a few days. She's a great young lady.

Lori called while Jeanna was here, "Sharon, I have some news for you."

Noticing her excitement, I guessed, "You're pregnant?"

"Yes."

I thought, *Just think—I'm going to be a grandma.*

In November, I attended a surprise party at Lori and David's house honoring Marge's seventieth birthday. I was nervous about attending. I felt sure it would be another tug-of-war with my emotions, but I also knew I wouldn't miss it. Since I believed that Marge had only told a select few of her friends about me, I feared it could be a difficult social situation.

Lori was radiant. Marge seemed happy to see us. My mom, my sister Betty, her son, and her granddaughter went with me. Lori and David had succeeded in keeping the party a surprise from Marge. Their house was nearly packed throughout the event.

David wasn't in the house when we first got there. Later, when he came into the living room and noticed me, he came over to see me. I stood up, and he gave me a hug and said, "It's good to see you again. I'm glad you could make it."

A man who had been sitting nearby stood up and started talking to David, saying, "You must be Lori's husband? I'm George, and I've known Marge since before she got married. I haven't seen her for a few years. We weren't able to come to your wedding. I remember when they adopted Lori. They were so happy. She was such a beautiful little girl."

Standing there with David and George, I heard George talk about Lori. Then, he said, "I live in Springfield."

Of all the people at that party I could have talked to, I was standing next to the one who also lived in Springfield. David then excused himself to talk to other guests, and I told George that I also lived in Springfield.

After a few minutes of small talk, George said, "If you live there, just how do you know Marge?"

I thought, *Okay, LORD, what am I going to do now?* I didn't want this day to be uncomfortable for Marge while she was with her friends, nor could I lie. I explained, "You just told David that you remembered when Lori was adopted. Well, I'm her birth mom."

George's mouth dropped.

While George was trying to think of something to say, I started rambling about Lori. Revealing how she had found me in 1995, I said, "The past few years have been the best years of my life, and I just love Marge."

George then gathered his composure, saying, "Here, I want you to meet my wife." Turning to his wife, he introduced me, "This is Sharon. She's Lori's birth mom." She wanted to hear more.

Marge then came over and asked, "Do you all know each other since you're all from Springfield?"

"We didn't before, but he came over while David was talking to me," I replied.

With her arm around me, Marge turned to George's wife and said, "This is Sharon, Lori's birth mom."

This time, my mouth dropped.

Making such a kind gesture was a big step. They all seemed thrilled to meet me. George's wife said, "She's so beautiful. You must be so proud of her."

A little later, my family and I left. We looked for Marge to say goodbye. My mom said, "I just had my eighty-fifth birthday last week. I told Sharon that I want an open house just like this for my ninetieth birthday."

Marge replied, "I'll be there to help you celebrate."

We then found Lori on the front porch greeting guests and saying goodbye to others. Giving me a big hug, she said, "I'm sorry I didn't really have time to spend with you. I'm so happy you came. Did you and George already know each other since you're both from Springfield?"

"No." I then explained the circumstances of having met George.

She said, "When I saw you talking to him, I was kind of panic-stricken not knowing how you and Mom would handle the situation. When I started planning the party, I just knew I wanted you there, not considering how difficult it might be for either of you. When I'm in Kansas City, I'm my mom's daughter. When I'm in Springfield, I'm known as your daughter."

"Your mom put her arm around me and introduced me as 'Sharon, Lori's birth mom.'"

Lori replied, "She said that?"

"Yes, she did."

Lori then said, "Just think, I was actually worried when I saw you both talking. I should have known the two of you could handle it and I needn't have worried."

As we left, I was overjoyed. In the van, I described what had taken place. Betty confirmed that Lori had seemed concerned about something. Mom said, "Sharon, you do know that this wasn't just a coincidence, don't you?"

"Yes, I know it was part of God's plan."

The closer it got to Christmas, I wondered if Bob had received Lori's e-mail message she sent to him in September. Was it possible it got lost in cyberspace? So that Lori and I wouldn't wonder about what might have happened, I mailed by restricted delivery a copy of her letter to Bob. I included an attached note, saying:

"Bob, I hadn't planned to ever contact you again, but I wanted to be sure you got Lori's e-mail message. I can't imagine anyone reading such a letter without responding. If you've read it and have decided not to respond, that's your decision. I'll abide by it. I just wanted to be sure you got it." As an afterthought, I added, "Lori is pregnant, and the baby's due in June."

Bob responded that he had received her e-mail, and he would respond to her directly if he made contact.

I replied, "Thanks for confirming you received Lori's letter. You never would have heard from me if you had confirmed receiving her e-mail in the first place. My original intent in providing Lori's address, e-mail, and telephone number was so that you wouldn't have to contact me again. I hope you have a Merry Christmas."

Immediately, I e-mailed Lori a copy of my note to Bob, a copy of his reply to me, and a copy of my final reply. With the possibility that Lori might have been upset with me, I said, "If you're upset with me, I hope that you can forgive me for contacting Bob."

Lori replied:

> I'm glad that you sent him the letter. I had been curious whether he had received it, but I'm not really concerned whether he makes contact. I'm sure he'll do whatever he feels is right. Let me know if you hear from him although I don't think you will from the tone of that letter. It's his loss! Thank you for contacting him. Love, Lori

becoming a grandma

Children's children are a crown to the aged,
and parents are the pride of their children.
(Proverbs 17:6, NIV)

*I*n February, Lori called to say, "According to the sonogram, we're going to have a boy. We're going to name him Joshua David."

I replied, "How exciting. I can't wait. Do you think you could come to Springfield for a baby shower? Evelyn and some of my friends would like to plan it."

Lori asked, "Is my mom invited? I'm not really sure that she would feel comfortable being in a situation where she doesn't know most of the guests."

"Yes, of course. Both your mom and Jeanna are invited."

Lori continued, "I asked my doctor if the hemorrhaging you suffered after my birth could be a hereditary concern for me. Although she didn't believe I had reason to be alarmed, I was wondering if you remember anything about your pregnancy that could help me. Would you send a request to the hospital to obtain your medical records?"

I assured her, "Of course, I will. I'm sorry that I don't remember more about my pregnancy or your birth." I was a little curious to see the records since I remembered very little about that time except that I had hemorrhaged.

After reading over my medical records, I was glad Lori had requested them. From the nurses' notes that were included, I learned I wasn't released from the hospital until the sixth day. My blood pressure dropped drastically after I started hemorrhaging shortly after Lori was born. The doctor was finally called at home a few hours later when the nurses became alarmed. Having been given a blood transfusion the first day and another pint the second day, I also received a lot of medication while I was there. Looking up the definition of the different medications given to me, I learned why I had little memory of that time. The purpose of one medication administered daily while I was there was to block waves to the brain to make me forget. I was sure Lori couldn't understand how I could forget something as important as the birth of a child. After she saw what was written in the nurses' notes, along with all of the medication I was given, she understood my memory loss.

Hearing from Lori almost daily the week before the baby shower was an enjoyable time for me. We had last-minute details to discuss. Lori was beginning to get a little apprehensive thinking about how many were going to attend the shower.

"Will it just be your family or also some friends?"

"I've invited my family, my long-time friends, my church friends, and my coworkers," I told her. Now why would she be apprehensive?

Twenty-three people attended the shower. Just before she

started opening the gifts, Lori said, "Now, Sharon, you'll have to write down the addresses for me so I can send thank-you notes." Showing her a sack containing preprinted address labels and some Snoopy thank-you cards that I had prepared for her, she smiled and said, "Of course, I should have known you would have everything under control."

Ron had flowers delivered to Marge at her home. He knew it took a lot of strength for her to attend the shower, and he wanted her to know how much we admired and loved her.

Marge replied, "It wasn't just Sharon who benefited and changed from her reunion with Lori. It worked both ways; Lori changed, too, all for the best."

After the shower, I was glowing. Actually, I hadn't stopped glowing since Lori and I met on February 11, 1995. Now all I had to do was to wait until my grandson made his debut.

Late one night in June, I received a call from Jeanna telling me Lori and David had left for the hospital. Hours later, I learned Josh had arrived shortly after midnight.

When I arrived at the hospital, I had a meaningful experience although I had missed the actual birth. While I was sitting there visiting with Lori, David, and Jeanna, the nurse came and said, "It's time to feed Josh."

Lori received instructions on how to breast-feed, and David learned how to change a diaper. What a priceless experience. The fact they felt comfortable enough with me to allow me to stay in the room during those sessions meant a lot to me. Becoming a grandma was a wonderful change for me, one I had never believed possible those twenty-five years before meeting Lori. I wondered what other changes could possibly be in store for me.

God's plans unfolding

All this is for your benefit, so that the grace that
is reaching more and more people may cause
thanksgiving to overflow to the glory of God.
(2 Corinthians 4:15, NIV)

*B*ecoming a grandma wasn't the only change for me
during 1999. The church I had joined in 1993 suffered
a major split. Many from my Sunday school class left,
including our teacher and her husband. To keep our class together,
we continued meeting in a private room at a grocery store. Finding
a church that we all felt comfortable in proved to be a struggle, and
we church-hopped for months.

Since Kathy was at the lake nearly every weekend, she joined
a church at the lake. She asked, "Are you any closer to making a
decision about joining a church?"

I replied, "Having a passion to help birth moms, I need to
find a church that can help me in that area." Knowing that not all

churches openly supported my passion, I changed my prayer soon after talking to Kathy. Instead of praying for what church was best for me, I asked Him for guidance in finding a church where I could serve Him the best. After I finished praying, I opened the brochure from the second church that I had been attending for many months. Listed on the back of the brochure was a list of ministries in which I could become involved.

Although I had received the brochure months before, I hadn't reviewed the list until that afternoon. Noticing an adoption-related ministry listed, I thought I could possibly be of some service there. I discussed the ministries with the pastor, and I sent him my web site address to briefly explain my interest. He told me about the local Pregnancy Care Center that was going to open after the New Year. He gave me the number of a church member who was also on the Board of Directors of the center, and she put me in touch with the director. The center was an indirect answer to my prayer for finding a church home.

I attended the center's first training class for volunteers, and I was asked to share my story. One of the instructors at the second training class told me, "I have to give you a hug. This week during a counseling session, one of my clients wouldn't open up. After telling her about your story and using your analogy of the turtle, she started opening up. Thank you for telling the story of your daughter and of how God is working in your life."

At a monthly get-together for the singles at my church in April of 2000, I spoke about my reunion with Lori. Since the date was getting nearer for the official opening of the Pregnancy Care Center, I told them about my involvement there. A number of people, male and female, came to me after I finished and thanked me for speaking. One young lady with tears in her eyes said, "I've been praying for God to guide me as far as getting involved in a mission. Until now, I hadn't received any direction. As soon as you began your story, I knew what I must do. I just work and do nothing after work except go home, so I have time to volunteer. I believe I could be of some use there." She was a labor and delivery nurse at the local hospital just across the street from the center. She immediately filled out a volunteer form.

During the evening services a week later, the pastor asked for anyone having anything to do with the Pregnancy Care Center to stand. He then asked those of us who stood to come to the front for special prayer. A lady came up and stood in front of me and started praying. She had her little boy with her. She and I were holding hands, and he was between us while she prayed. We had never met prior to this time, and she asked, "How are you connected to the center?"

I replied that I was a volunteer mentor and that I had been reunited with Lori for ten years. With tear-stained eyes, she shared, "I'm an adoptive mother of two boys. I've always hoped that I would be able to say thanks to the mother of my two boys. I had no idea why, but I felt the Lord nudging me to pray for someone. It is now clear why."

hope for a future

> "For I know the plans I have for you," declares the
> Lord, "plans to prosper you and not to harm you,
> plans to give you hope and a future."
> (Jeremiah 29:11, NIV)

*I*n January 2001, I spent a day with Lori and Josh. Just before
I was getting ready to leave, Lori asked, "It's his naptime. Do
you have to go or can you rock him to sleep?"

I replied, "Of course, I have the time." I rocked him and read to
him until he fell asleep. This was one time he didn't protest about
taking a nap.

Ron said, "Sharon, since you no longer hide under a shell of
protection, you're going to have to start a different collection."

The acrostic turtle's shell that I used earlier changed. Now, it
describes the way I see myself living under God's protection and
since meeting Lori:

TRANSFORMED–like a new person

UNCONDITIONAL LOVE–a new thing for me

RADIANT–beaming with joy

TRIUMPHANT–no longer in that shell syndrome

LONG-WINDED–my family can vouch for that

ECSTATIC–never been happier

SMILE–a glowing smile

SHELLABRATE–rejoicing in God's glory

HOPE–having hope for a future

EXCITEMENT–filled with cheerfulness

LIBERTY–no longer in that bondage

LUMINOUS–shining when I mention my daughter

On Mother's Day 2001, I spoke at Ron's church for its Mother's Day services. Since I had spoken there in 1998, I was honored to be asked to return and finish the rest of the story. This time, my story included my involvement with the Pregnancy Care Center, my grandson, and the anticipation of my granddaughter's birth. I left for the hospital in Kansas City after the service.

Every Mother's Day has been special since Lori found me in 1995, but this year topped them all. When I arrived at the hospital and started down the hall, I heard, "Josh, there's your Grandma Sharon." He was with his other two grandmothers. After a few hugs and discussing the birth of our granddaughter, we all went to the nursery. There, we got to see Rhiannon. Words cannot describe the excitement when I saw Rhiannon for the first time. Then, we went to the room to see Lori and David. What a special Mother's Day.

Our individual personalities make us unique. My personality is the type that normally keeps things closed and inside. I am grateful for being able to open up and share this exciting part of my life.

After sharing my story as a volunteer mentor at the Pregnancy Care Center, I was asked by a client, "Do you have any regrets? I'm afraid that I'll have too many regrets if I choose adoption. What if I chose adoption and then won the lottery? I would then be able to care for my child, but it would be too late."

I asked, "What if you don't win the lottery? Placing a baby for adoption isn't easy, but neither is parenting a child alone. None of your options will be easy. Base your decisions upon what you think is best for your child and what you can live with, not what someone else wants for you. Having felt that I did what was best for my daughter, I just want to be sure you're fully informed on all of your options."

Regrets? Yes, I have regrets:

1. Fearing their reactions, I regret I hid my feelings from my friends and family.

2. Since I never married or had any more children during those years, I regret I vowed not to let anyone get close to me again.

3. Many years were wasted feeling estranged from God. Because I believe that my hurts and struggles happened for a reason, I don't dwell on those regrets. That reason is promised in Jeremiah 29:11.

How can I have regrets about making a plan of adoption for my baby when I consider the wonderful life Lori had? Seeing her beautiful smile, I know that I had a big part in that smile. Had I chosen to parent her alone, she might not have had so many things to smile about. I'm thankful for the opportunity of getting to know and love her, her husband, and her precious children. Trying not to question why things turn out the way they do, I have to rely on knowing there is a reason for everything.

beauty, not ashes

The Spirit of the Sovereign LORD is on me, because the
LORD has anointed me to preach good news to the poor.
He has sent me to bind up the brokenhearted, to proclaim
freedom for the captives and release from darkness for the
prisoners, to proclaim the year of the LORD's favor and the
day of vengeance of our God, to comfort all who mourn, and
provide for those who grieve in Zion—to bestow on them a
crown of beauty instead of ashes, the oil of gladness instead
of mourning, and a garment of praise instead of a spirit of
despair. They will be called oaks of righteousness, a planting
of the LORD for the display of his splendor.
(Isaiah 61:1–3, NIV)

*I*n May 2002, I retired as police services administrator after
working with the local police department for twenty-eight
years. The department had a retirement party for me. Lori,
Marge, Josh, and Rhiannon were there with me. I was thrilled they
were there to share that important day with me.

Another big change, a devastating change, happened during 2003—My mom became ill and was hospitalized with congestive heart failure. She died two months later; eight months prior to what would have been her ninetieth birthday. I was so thankful I had retired the previous year and was able to spend more quality time with her during her last year of life.

Lori and Marge brought Josh and Rhiannon to see Mom after she was first released from the hospital. Mom loved spending time with Lori since that first day we were reunited. Although she was ill, she thoroughly enjoyed spending the day with them. Lori and Marge sat beside me at Mom's funeral. Their support meant a lot to me.

Mom was one of my greatest supporters for getting this story written. She proofed my first draft and frequently encouraged me to get it published. She was always eager to go with me to hear me share my story publicly.

After her death, my goal of spending more time at the Pregnancy Care Center was accomplished. I was hired by the center on a part-time basis as the client services assistant. I continued speaking on behalf of the center and sharing my story at every opportunity.

In 2003, Judy Mills contacted me. She is an adult adoptee who found and was reunited with her birth siblings. Her birth mom died a year earlier. Together, we started the Adoption Triad of the Ozarks, a group that meets monthly to offer support to anyone who has been touched by adoption.[5]

Several speaking opportunities came my way in 2004. A birth mom friend and I taught a workshop at the annual conference in Kansas City of the American Adoption Congress. Lori was there with me while I spoke. A few weeks later, I attended the Infant Adoption Awareness Training Program of the National Council for Adoption. On the last day of that training, a panel of birth moms in open adoptions answered questions. I was then asked to share my story, depicting quite a contrast shown in closed adoptions. Great strides have been made in adoptions from the closed adoption era of the sixties. Some agencies now offer life-time counseling for birth moms, a much needed improvement over the brief counseling I received in 1969: "Going on with your life and forgetting about this part of it would be the best thing for you."

A summation of my story, "Mother's Day—A New Beginning," was published in the May–July 2004 issue of Caring magazine.[6]

A few months later, I shared my story during a workshop in Charlotte, North Carolina, at the annual Heartbeat International Conference. I was invited to share with centers across the nation how they can become more adoption friendly.

I haven't mentioned my speaking engagements to bring attention to myself but to show the kind of healing that can take place when sharing with others. Instead of staying under that shell of protection, I prefer to tell the world the awesome change that has resulted from being reunited with my daughter.

The year 2004 also brought some other awesome experiences. I spent time with Josh and Rhiannon at their birthday celebrations along with their other grandmothers and family members. Spending Grandparent's Day with Josh at his school was more than I ever dreamed possible. He introduced me to his teacher and classmates by saying, "This is my Grandma Sharon. She likes to buy me toys, and she collects turtles." That night I went out to eat with Lori, David, Josh, Rhiannon, and Marge. I spent the night with Marge at her house and slept in the room that was Lori's when she was growing up. Marge and I spent time looking at photos and talking about Lori.

Later in December, my friend Roger and I attended a day set

aside for family members and friends to watch Rhiannon and her friends at dance practice preparing for a dance recital.

February 2, 2005 marked the ten-year anniversary of receiving the most important telephone call of my life: the day I learned that Lori wanted to meet me. I have been blessed during the ten years with getting to see her about every other month.

Another highlight of 2005 came when Lori agreed to be a part of our quarterly volunteer update meetings at the Pregnancy Care Center. Our focus was on adoption from an adoptee's viewpoint. Lori and three of my friends who are adult adoptees shared stories about their lives and then answered questions. Lori was asked if she had met her birth father. She replied that seven years had passed since she e-mailed a letter to him. Although he acknowledged her letter, he has chosen not to meet her. She felt he had the right to his decision and she respected his decision, but she felt it was his loss. Josh and Rhiannon came with Lori, and they stayed at my house. Rhiannon told me when they arrived, "Grandma Sharon, we're going to have two sleepovers at your house." Just before they left, she told me, "Grandma Sharon, we're going to come back and have five sleepovers at your house." I can hardly wait.

The year 2005 ended with a huge change. Roger, my friend of several years, and I chose to get married in a small intimate wedding ceremony in the presence of our children: my daughter, her family, and Roger's two sons Bryan and Chris. My life is now complete with a husband, a daughter and her husband, two sons, and three grandchildren Josh, Rhiannon, and Roger "R2" Romaine.

18

freedom to choose

In him we were also chosen, having been predestined
according to the plan of him who works out
everything in conformity with the purpose of his will,
in order that we, who were the first to hope in Christ,
might be for the praise of his glory."
(Ephesians 1:11–12, NIV)

God's plan for my life has included sharing this story with you. Each time I share this story, whether in a public or a private setting, another layer of healing takes place. Life is made up of choices we make each day. Without having chosen God to be a part of my life, I feel certain this book would have had an entirely different ending. He gave me the free will to choose Him and to make other choices. I'm glad that I chose life for my baby in 1969. I'm also grateful that I chose to make a plan of adoption for her so she could have a better life than the one I felt I could provide. I don't downplay or minimize that feeling of loss all of those years; instead, I choose to focus on the joys I've received because of that choice. I could focus on the inner struggle and pain that was involved in making that plan of adoption; instead, I choose each day to think of my daughter and grandchildren and to smile.

endnotes

1. Towns, Jim, Ph. D. *Single Space, Victorious Living for the Single Adult*, 1990, published by Honor Books. 67.

2. Stearns, Ann Kaiser. *Living Through Personal Crisis*, 132, 1984. Ballantine Books, a Division of Random House, Inc.

3. Overstreet, Sarah (1997), Associate Editorial Page Editor. "From a shell, heart emerges." *News-Leader*, Sunday, May 11, 1997. Reprinted by permission of the Springfield (Mo.) News-Leader.

4. Agee, Linda, (1997), Letter to editor concerning "OVER-STREET: Subject of column definition of strength." *News-Leader*, Monday, May 19, 1997. Reprinted by permission of the Springfield (Mo.) News-Leader.

5. Adoption Triad of the Ozarks, P. O. Box 505, Springfield, MO 65801–0505.

6. Fieker, Sharon, (2004), "Mother's Day—A New Beginning." *Caring—A Guide to the Benevolences Ministries of the Assemblies of God*, May-July 2004.

TATE PUBLISHING & *Enterprises*

Tate Publishing is committed to excellence in the publishing industry. Our staff of highly trained professionals, including editors, graphic designers, and marketing personnel, work together to produce the very finest books available. The company reflects the philosophy established by the founders, based on Psalms 68:11,

"THE LORD GAVE THE WORD AND GREAT WAS THE COMPANY OF THOSE WHO PUBLISHED IT."

If you would like further information, please call
1.888.361.9473
or visit our website
www.tatepublishing.com

TATE PUBLISHING & *Enterprises*, LLC
127 E. Trade Center Terrace
Mustang, Oklahoma 73064 USA